FINDING CHRIST
IN THE COVENANT PATH

ANCIENT INSIGHTS FOR MODERN LIFE

JENNIFER C. LANE

Published by the Religious Studies Center, Brigham Young University, Provo, Utah, in cooperation with Deseret Book Company, Salt Lake City, Utah.
Visit us at rsc.byu.edu.

© 2020 by Brigham Young University. All rights reserved.

Printed in the United States of America by Sheridan Books, Inc.

DESERET BOOK is a registered trademark of Deseret Book Company.
Visit us at DeseretBook.com.

Any uses of this material beyond those allowed by the exemptions in US copyright law, such as section 107, "Fair Use," and section 108, "Library Copying," require the written permission of the publisher, Religious Studies Center, 185 HGB, Brigham Young University, Provo, UT 84602. The views expressed herein are the responsibility of the authors and do not necessarily represent the position of Brigham Young University or the Religious Studies Center.

Cover and interior design by Emily V. Strong.

ISBN 978-1-9443-9490-5

Library of Congress Cataloging-in-Publication Data

Names: Lane, Jennifer C., 1968- author.
Title: Finding Christ in the covenant path : ancient insights for modern life / Jennifer C. Lane.
Description: Provo, Utah : Religious Studies Center, Brigham Young University : Salt Lake City, Utah : in cooperation with Deseret Book Company, [2020] | Includes bibliographical references and index. | Summary: "Through a study of both biblical terms and medieval images, this volume offers fresh insights to coming unto Christ through the process of making and keeping covenants. With personal anecdotes, historical background, and scriptural analysis by the author, this book explores the doctrine of walking the covenant path and teaches how to behold Christ more fully in the ordinances"-- Provided by publisher.
Identifiers: LCCN 2019040228 | ISBN 9781944394905 (hardcover)
Subjects: LCSH: Jesus Christ--Mormon interpretations. | Church of Jesus Christ of Latter-day Saints--Doctrines. | Worship--History. | Mormon Church--Doctrines.
Classification: LCC BX8643.J4 L36 2020 | DDC 232.088/2893--dc23
LC record available at https://lccn.loc.gov/2019040228

CONTENTS

Acknowledgments — V

Introduction — VII

PART ONE: **CHRIST, OUR KINSMAN-REDEEMER**

1. Exploring Ancient Words — 3
2. Covenant (*bĕrît*) — 7
3. Redemption (*gāʾal*) — 17
4. Worship (*ḥwh* and *ʿābad*) — 35
5. The Presence of the Lord (*pānîm*) — 45
6. Sitting Enthroned (*yāšab*) — 61

PART TWO: **CHRIST, OUR RANSOM PRICE**

7. Exploring Medieval Images — 77
8. The Image of Christ — 85
9. Relics — 95
10. *Arma Christi* — 109

CONTENTS

11. The Winepress — 119

12. Pietá — 129

13. Man of Sorrows — 145

14. Stigmata — 153

PART THREE: CONCLUSION

15. Covenants and the True Vine — 173

For Further Reading — 179

Index — 183

Acknowledgments

I am grateful to Lisa Roper at Deseret Book and the staff at the Religious Studies Center at Brigham Young University for all their help through the publication process. The RSC publications director, Scott C. Esplin, a fellow student of pilgrimage and piety, was open and encouraging to the idea of a devotional book rooted in scholarship from the first contact that we had. Brent R. Nordgren, RSC production and business supervisor, helped move everything forward quickly, including assisting me with the technical aspect of the images. I also owe a debt to the anonymous peer reviewers who provided very helpful suggestions.

Shirley S. Ricks, senior editor, provided expert editorial suggestions and was always collaborative and thoughtful in talking through different issues. I am also grateful to the intern, Sarah Whitney Johnson, who was so careful in working through the initial manuscript and giving me very helpful suggestions. Emily V. Strong's creative work with the design of the book transcended what I could have ever imagined the final product to be.

ACKNOWLEDGMENTS

I celebrate the influence of my mother, M. Roxanne Watkins Clark, in several places throughout this volume; the role of my father, Nolan Ezra Clark, is less heralded but no less significant. I learned the value of biblical word studies as he explained the Hebrew term for *honor* in Exodus 20:12 from his well-used *Strong's Exhaustive Concordance of the Bible*; I wanted to live to bring "weight" to the name of my parents from his teaching. His consistent pattern of early morning scripture study and early Saturday morning temple attendance modeled a life of serious discipleship. The faithfulness and devotion to God I experienced in my home rooted and grounded me in spiritual reality from my earliest memories.

My brother, Jonathan Clark, and one of my mission companions were among the earliest readers, and I am so grateful for their support and encouragement. Elizabeth Clark, my sister, and my cousin Rebecca Clark Carey were careful readers and editors through the writing process, and without their suggestions, feedback, and encouragement, I would not have had the courage to keep going.

I am grateful to Brigham Young University–Hawaii for granting me a sabbatical during Fall Semester 2018. I am grateful to the library staff at the Harold B. Lee Library for providing me with a research room during that time. I am also grateful to all my colleagues at BYU–Hawaii who covered classes during that semester.

For many years, maybe decades, my husband, Keith Lane, along with my sister and a dear friend, Lisa Rosenbaum Ishikuro, have all urged me to write my research insights on redemption for a larger audience. I am grateful for their encouragement and support.

I am particularly grateful to Keith who, from the earliest days of our married life through today, has graciously shared his life and time with me and my research and writing. Since we first met we have shared a love of both religious studies and gospel study. Having our path together include a shared professional life has been a great blessing. His love and support have both kept me grounded and given me space to explore and learn.

INTRODUCTION

We feel lost. We are trapped. But our Heavenly Father has a plan. He wants us to know that his plan of redemption will work. We are not supposed to stay lost and in bondage, separated from his presence. His plan is big enough to bring all his children home. He has chosen his Only Begotten Son as our Redeemer, the one who gave his life to ransom us from our captivity and to bring us back through the covenant path. This message of hope is communicated in scriptures and in the ordinances we perform, particularly in the temple.

But we have a problem. Much of the language of scripture is rooted in an ancient world, a world of relationships and symbols that can feel foreign. The plan of redemption and its covenants are expressed in ancient words that we are filtering through modern eyes and ears. We hear the words but don't always understand the message of hope that our Father is trying so hard to communicate. The assurance of our ransom price is likewise communicated through symbols in the ordinances that we can easily tune out or rush by in our hectic modern lives.

This book has two parts to help bring into focus this message of Christ as our Redeemer and as our Ransom. The first part helps us see Christ's identity as our Kinsman-Redeemer by exploring the ancient words that connect covenants, redemption, worship, the presence of the Lord, and sitting down enthroned in God's presence as his children and heirs. The second part helps us see Christ as our Ransom by exploring medieval images that can help us increase our confidence in the price that was paid for our deliverance. Christ invites us to "behold the wounds which pierced my side, and also the prints of the nails in my hands and feet" (Doctrine and Covenants 6:37). Knowing that he is our Redeemer and that his suffering and death is our ransom price allows us to "look unto [him] in every thought" and to "doubt not" and "fear not" (Doctrine and Covenants 6:36).

This is the message our Father in Heaven has been trying so hard to communicate to us—Christ can free us and bring us home if we trust him and come unto him. Learning from ancient words and medieval images can provide additional tools to help us tune in to this message of hope. With these additional resources, we can study the scriptures and participate in the ordinances with deeper and deeper experiences of God's love and assurance. We can more fully rely on our Redeemer and more fully come unto him, receiving the gift of life that he offers us.

This journey of coming unto Christ can be understood more clearly as we become attuned to the concepts and symbolic language communicated in the covenants and ordinances of salvation. These covenants and ordinances, including those of the temple, map out this journey back to the presence of God through the redemption of Jesus Christ. Our understanding of this journey of our life becomes clearer as we learn the meaning of ancient words that connect covenants, redemption, and returning to God's presence to sit enthroned. Likewise, learning to ponder images and symbols pointing to Christ's suffering and death can open our eyes and minds to more clearly behold the symbolic presentation throughout the ordinances. A deeper study of these ancient words allows us to appreciate the power of our covenant relationship with Christ, and a deeper study of medieval devotional images gives us practice in pondering the images of Christ's suffering and death, allowing us to see the message of redeeming love communicated in the ordinances.

Part one, "Christ, Our Kinsman-Redeemer," develops core scriptural concepts to explain why faith in Christ and making and keeping covenants can bring peace and hope to all. With explanations and personal accounts, it develops the ancient sense in which covenants (bĕrît) create family relationships. It explains that Christ's role as our Kinsman-Redeemer (gō'ēl), the Hebrew role of one appointed to buy family members out of bondage, stems from those relationships. We can have confidence that he is our Redeemer because of our covenants with him.

When we feel Christ's redeeming love and forgiveness, we are free. Understanding ancient concepts of being freed from bondage to live lives of worship (ḥwḥ and ʿābad, literally "bowing down" and "serving") helps us reconcile ourselves to living as the Lord's servants, expressing our gratitude for redemption. We learn to trust him and are increasingly willing to walk in his ways, even when we don't understand them. Old Testament temple symbolism shows how covenant worship brings us to the presence of the Lord (pānîm). Understanding the multiple meanings of the phrase *the presence of the Lord* reminds us that we can experience his presence in this life as well as in the eternities, which encourages us to seek for holiness—the sanctification of thoughts and actions through Christ.

As we continue following the journey of this covenant path, we learn that the Lord invites us to sit down on his throne (yāšab). He wants us to experience his kind of life now and forever. When we despair that we can never become what we have promised to be, he reminds us of his power to redeem and exalt. Our covenants bring us into his family, allowing him as our Kinsman-Redeemer to redeem us. We need to understand the power of these covenants with our Redeemer to escape from any bondage that we experience. Through trusting in his redeeming love, we live lives of worship, find joy in holiness, and experience the presence of God now and forever.

Part two, "Christ, Our Ransom Price," also draws on a different cultural frame of reference to provide additional tools for tuning in to familiar gospel symbols from the scriptures and temple. With personal anecdotes, historical background, and scriptural analysis, this section uses devotional images and late medieval practices of contemplation as a strategy to help us more fully accept the Savior's invitation to "behold the wounds" (Doctrine and Covenants 6:37) and to "behold the sufferings and death of him who did no sin" (Doctrine and Covenants 45:4). By using medieval images as a counterpoint to Restoration practices and ordinances, we can more fully appreciate the gift that has been given and see it with fresh eyes.

This part of the book explores the use and limits of devotional images, particularly the image of Christ. In addition to exploring the role of devotional images in the Middle Ages, this section also gives some general background to help us see how the physical can connect us with Christ. In the early Christian period the tombs of martyrs were a sacred space for believers, and in time that role was served by the saints' bodies, which could be transported to new places, thus bringing the holiness of the saints to others as relics. Later we see the rise of passion (Atonement-related) relics as the focus on Christ's mortal life became more central in the later Middle Ages. This desire to be close to the sacred can be seen in the emphasis on restoring and visiting sacred places of Church history such as Palmyra, Kirtland, and Nauvoo, but more importantly, this yearning also points to the broader potential for physical connection with the sacred through ordinances.

The devotional imagery known as the *Arma Christi*, symbols of the events of the passion, was a medieval visual strategy to focus meditation on Christ's atoning suffering and death. Learning from the practice of meditating on the *Arma Christ* helps us to slow down and ponder Christ's ransom price for us. Developing this focus can help us draw more out of our time with both the scriptures and the ordinances. Another devotional image of Christ's suffering is the image of him treading the winepress, which draws on descriptions in both Isaiah and the book of Revelation. This depiction of Christ's gift of suffering for us can be seen in imagery tied in to both olive oil and the sacrament. The image of Christ with his garments red from treading the winepress alone helps us understand our need to receive the gift of his ransom price, lest it turn to witness against us.

The widely known image of the Pietà provides a way to think about how others' responses to Christ's suffering and death can help us learn to respond to him. Late medieval texts and images modeled responses to Christ and helped people know how to respond to him. While we may not ever have these kinds of visual reminders, our daily study of the Book of Mormon can also provide us with powerful textual examples of people whose response to Christ was life changing.

A lesser-known late medieval image of Christ is the Man of Sorrows, also known as the *Imago pietatis*, which captures the image both of Christ's suffering and also of his resurrection. The importance of appreciating both aspects of his Atonement can be seen by Christ's focus on his wounds in his postresurrection appearances. Bringing his atoning death and infinite life together in our minds increases our faith in his redeeming power.

The last chapter of this section explores how, as we come unto Christ, we can fully receive this ransom price by receiving the image of Christ in ourselves. The idea of taking on Christ's image in a physical sense is explored by engaging with the image of St. Francis, his life of discipleship, and his stigmata and what this example points to about embodied knowledge. The idea of knowing Christ through the ordinances as well as in our lives is critical to receiving the redemption that we have been offered. When we see knowledge as more than information—as a way of being that is modeled and enacted in the ordinances—we can more fully appreciate living at a time when the knowledge and redeeming power of the Lord are being poured out more fully than ever before.

INTRODUCTION

As our vision opens up to what we are being offered through the covenants and ordinances, we can more fully receive them in our lives. As we behold the gift of his love and sacrifice, we can more fully receive Christ into our lives. The covenants and ordinances offer both the message and the power of redemption. Christ is inviting us to come unto him, and as we accept that invitation and embark on that journey, we find in him the life, light, and hope that the Father is trying so hard to share with us.

PART ONE

CHRIST, OUR KINSMAN-REDEEMER

We come unto Christ through the covenant path. Marianne von Werefkin, The Way of the Cross II, 1921. Museo Comunale d'Arte Moderna, Asconda. Permission granted by Cutler Miles Art Gallery, cutlermiles.com. © Cutler Miles Art Gallery.

CHAPTER 1

EXPLORING ANCIENT WORDS

t shouldn't have been a surprise that the inspiration would come through music. As I was growing up in Arlington, Virginia, many moments of revelation and personal testimony came as I sang. As a young teenager singing an Easter Cantata with the ward choir, I felt the reality of the account in the lyrics that "very early in the morning, on the first day of the week, the women came to the sepulchre" and found that he was not here, but "was risen as they said." A couple years later "A Poor Wayfaring Man of Grief" was the closing hymn in a meeting where Elder Oaks had given an apostolic blessing. As I sang, I felt it was my own witness that "the tokens in his hands I knew; the Savior stood before mine eyes."[1]

In my first year away from home, I sang the Duruflé Requiem with the Wellesley College Choir in Massachusetts, and tears fell from my eyes when I sang, "Agnus Dei, qui tollis peccata mundi," and I received an additional witness that, as the text said, Christ was indeed the Lamb of God who had taken upon himself the sin of the world. A couple years later when I was in the Missionary Training Center, Elder Haight shared the experience of his vision of Christ on the cross that he had received while he was seriously unwell, and we then sang "I Believe in Christ." I had to get tissues from the missionaries around me during the hymn because I was crying so hard from the witness I felt as I sang, "I believe in Christ; he ransoms me. From Satan's grasp he sets me free."[2]

So on a car trip with my family a year after returning from my mission to France, it wasn't a surprise that I felt a spiritual witness and confirmation while singing about the Savior, but this time there was an additional impression. It was just after the end of the summer term at Brigham Young University, where I had transferred just before my sophomore year. At the end of my first year at school after my misison, I had gone home to Virginia for a short trip up to Church history sites with my parents and younger brother, who was preparing to start school at BYU that fall.

Our family had a "Christmas in August" tradition, and we were singing Christmas carols as we drove on August 25. As we sang the second verse of the carol "Far, Far Away on Judea's Plains," the words "sweet are these strains of redeeming love, message of mercy from heav'n above" brought with them a powerful spirit.[3] I felt an overwhelming confirmation of the reality of Christ's redeeming love and also a sense that this was the topic for my thesis.

On that car trip I was looking ahead to my last year at BYU. I was a history major and would be writing an honors thesis that year. I had had a sense for a while that this was important and that I needed to give thought to what I should write about. Since my mission, I was looking for topics, focusing on religious history in my classes and papers, hoping to narrow my studies and to find something to pursue, but nothing had stood out so far.

Earlier that summer I worked as a custodian at the Missionary Training Center cafeteria after breakfast. Day after day, I pushed the vacuum along the carpet of the quiet dining halls, cleaning up Cap'n Crunch cereal crumbs and singing to myself, offering a prayer in my heart that the right topic would come.

When the impression about which topic to write on came while I was singing in the car, I was fortunate to have a notebook computer with an early version of scripture search software. I opened it up to do some research. I needed to find out just what redemption was and where it was found in the scriptures. As I searched, I realized—to my surprise—that terms related to redemption and redeem showed up overwhelmingly in the Old Testament, quite often in the Book of Mormon, and a few times in the New Testament and Doctrine and Covenants.

When I got back to Provo I made an appointment to talk with Stephen Ricks, a professor of Hebrew and one of the associate deans of the honors program, about working with me as my advisor on an ancient Near Eastern topic. He initially encouraged me to read a book about each of the major ancient Near Eastern civilizations and then to come back and talk about what I wanted to focus on. I dutifully went and looked at a number of books, but a week later I came back and finally had the courage to tell him that I wanted to study redemption in the ancient Near East and Old Testament.

His willing support gave me the courage to dig in. I studied the scholarship of key terms associated with redemption. I printed out all the scriptures with *redemption* or *redeem* in the Old Testament. I studied each of the passages in the Book of Mormon where these terms were found. Then one day, as I sat in the library and looked through the scripture printouts, something clicked. I started to see a pattern and a connection between *redemption* and *covenant*. In the Old Testament the Lord Jehovah is the Redeemer of Israel. In my studies I started to understand why and what that meant for them and for me.

This academic journey led to not only an honors thesis but also a publication in the *Journal of Book of Mormon Studies*[4] and a presentation and publication in the following year's Sperry Symposium volume. Twelve years later that article was chosen for inclusion in *Sperry Symposium Classics: The Old Testament*, a collection of past articles dealing with topics from the Old Testament.⁵ My academic journey to understand redemption and the Lord's role as our Redeemer also led to a master's thesis on New Testament aspects of the theme and, over the years, several additional publications on dimensions of this topic related to the New Testament, Book of Mormon, Pearl of Great Price, and Doctrine and Covenants. As a professor of religious education at BYU–Hawaii, I have had the chance to do additional word studies and publications on other ancient words and phrases with deep and relevant meanings: *worship, the presence of God,* and *sitting down enthroned.* These words and concepts, understood in their ancient setting, weave together with the concepts of covenant and redemption to describe our covenant path back to God.

I will always be grateful for the witness I felt as I sang "the song of redeeming love" that summer on a family car trip along the East Coast (Alma 5:26). The journey of my life has been interwoven with the concepts that I have learned. Sometimes the experiences helped me to see the concepts and sometimes the concepts helped me to live through the experiences. I am grateful for the privilege to have spent so much of my life combining academic and personal study of the gospel. The love and witness I have felt through these studies has guided my life; I would like to share some of what I have learned with you here.

Notes

1. James Montgomery, "A Poor Wayfaring Man of Grief," in *Hymns* (Salt Lake City: The Church of Jesus Christ of Latter-day Saints, 1985), no. 29.

2. Bruce R. McConkie, "I Believe in Christ," in *Hymns*, no. 134.

3. John M. Macfarlane, "Far, Far Away on Judea's Plains," in *Hymns*, no. 212.

4. Jennifer C. Lane, "The Lord Will Redeem His People: 'Adoptive' Covenant and Redemption in the Old Testament and the Book of Mormon," *Journal of Book of Mormon Studies* 2, no. 2 (1993): 39–62.

5. Jennifer C. Lane, "The Lord Will Redeem His People: Adoptive Covenant and Redemption in the Old Testament," in *Sperry Symposium Classics: The Old Testament,* ed. Paul Y. Hoskisson (Salt Lake City: Deseret Book; and Provo, UT: Religious Studies Center, Brigham Young University, 2005), 298–310.

CHAPTER 2

COVENANT

bĕrît

hen I was in graduate school in Southern California, I served in our ward's Primary presidency. It was my responsibility to visit children as they were turning eight years old to help them learn more about baptism and the gift of the Holy Ghost. The presidency had put together a small packet of visual aids to explain how we experience the Holy Ghost—a little birthday candle for the light we feel, a tiny little blanket for the comfort we feel, and so on. It was harder to explain covenants, but the language used in the presentation to talk about the covenant of baptism made sense to an eight-year-old: We make promises to God, and he makes promises to us. We know that we have obligations to him, and we know that he has obligations to us. He binds himself to us based on our obedience (see Doctrine and Covenants 82:10).

As we get older, this simple concept of promises gets layered with our adult life experiences. We sign contracts for phones, apartments, cars, mortgages, and so on. We have obligations to make payment in exchange

We begin to take Christ's name upon us as we start on the covenant path.

for goods and services. We do our part, and we expect the other party to do their part. We make contracts. We break contracts. Others break contracts. We are penalized for breaking contracts, but that's part of life.

This contractual model can and does easily color our sense of what *covenant* means. But in the ancient world, making a covenant wasn't a matter of commerce. In ancient Israel the term for *covenant* was *běrît*. The concept behind *běrît* is a relationship, understood as a family relationship. Making a covenant in scriptural terms can best be understood as forming a new relationship.

When we get married we create a new relationship. When we adopt a child we create a new relationship. There are promises that we make to each other, but this is not a contract. We are creating new families. We are different people in these new relationships. We become husbands and wives, parents and children.

Covenants create family relationships. Covenants change who we are because they change our relationship with those around us and their relationship to us.

We intuitively understand the changes in identity that come with marriage and parenthood; that is shown in part by the change of name that often accompanies marriage and adoption. We are in a new relationship, and we are different than we were before. There is a new sense of family identity.

New Family Relationships

In ancient Israel this sense of covenants as creating new family relationships not only brought people together with each other but also brought them together with the Lord. They became his people, and he became their God. In the Old Testament we also see names change as part of making a covenant relationship with the Lord. For example, when the Lord appeared to Abram, he told him that he was "the Almighty God" and that he had expectations for Abram: "walk before me and be thou perfect ['whole, without blemish']," but these expectations were part of a new relationship that he was establishing. "*I will make my covenant between me and thee, and will multiply thee exceedingly. And Abram fell on his face: and God talked with him, saying, As for me, behold, my covenant is with thee, and thou shalt be a father of many nations. Neither shall thy name any more be called Abram, but thy name shall be Abraham; for a father of many nations have I made thee*" (Genesis 17:1–5; emphasis added). To emphasize the new relationship of covenant, the Lord said again, "I will establish my covenant between me and thee and thy seed . . . to be a God unto thee, and to thy seed after thee" (Genesis 17:7). A new name was given and a new relationship established.

Abram became Abraham. Sarai became Sarah. Jacob became Israel. In the ancient world, names were serious business. They were understood to reflect something of a person's true nature as well as their relationship to others. So, changing names would be a natural extension of creating a new relationship by covenant. The word for *name* in Hebrew (šēm, pronounced *shem*) can also be translated as "remembrance" or "memorial." It is a marker to oneself and to others. This new name pointed to a new reality. Abram, "exalted father," became Abraham, "father of a multitude," through covenant promise. While it took years for that reality to appear, this covenant name and promise was the foundation for his faithfully continuing on the path.

We can see the Lord using covenants to create a new family relationship with individuals in the era of the patriarchs and also with all of Israel through the covenant made at the time of Moses. By making a collective covenant with the Lord at Mount Sinai, the people of Israel entered into his family and protection. We can see the language of adoption being used when the Lord tells Moses, "I will take you to me for a people, and I will be to you a God" (Exodus 6:7).

In the Book of Mormon, we see these same ancient patterns. The people of King Benjamin are told that they have also entered into a new family relationship because of their willingness to covenant with the Lord. King Benjamin explained that "because of the covenant which ye have made ye shall be called the children of Christ, his sons, and his daughters; for behold, this day he hath spiritually begotten you; for ye say that your hearts are changed through faith on his name; therefore, ye are born of him and have become his sons and his daughters" (Mosiah 5:7). They likewise received a new name in association with their new covenant relationship. "I would that ye should take upon you the name of Christ, all you that have entered into the covenant with God that ye should be obedient unto the end of your lives" (5:8). Covenants create family relationships that are marked by a new name, reflecting a new nature.

For King Benjamin's people, taking the name of Christ as a covenant name indicated a new relationship, a new identity, and the promise of a new nature created by their covenant. Just as Abraham did not become a "father of a multitude" immediately upon entering into the covenant relationship, taking upon us the name of Christ is part of the covenant promise of what we can become through covenant faithfulness.

These concepts about covenants are simple but have profound implications. The restoration of priesthood keys in this last dispensation occurred precisely to enable us to make covenants with the Lord. A covenant can't be just a promise to him to be good. Throughout millennia, many people have tried very hard to be good and to follow God as best they can. A covenant is a new relationship created by one who has authority to speak for the Lord, whose covenant it is. A covenant binds us to God and binds God to us. A covenant makes us part of Christ's family; we become "the children of Christ, his sons, and his daughters" (Mosiah 5:7).

Covenants speak to the question of identity, something that we may struggle with throughout our lives in different times and contexts. We try to understand ourselves and our nature. We first look to our parents to find out who we are. This can be a struggle as we grow up and come to recognize their weaknesses as well as their strengths. We want to hope that we can measure up to the good in preceding generations and escape from the traps that we may have inherited. We may, however, feel trapped in multigenerational patterns of pride or fear or anger, family patterns that can often feel as though they define us and lock us into a way of being.

When we meditate on the covenant relationship and promises of baptism, the endowment, and temple marriage, we should see ourselves becoming more and more connected to the Lord. Our covenants with God open us up to new potential and new identity. We need to recognize that through making these covenants we become his. We are part of his family. Covenant promises give us the vision that our reality is bigger than our past choices or our present self-assessment. Covenant promises show us that we are not who we thought we were. Because we have entered into these covenant relationships with the Lord God of Israel and taken his name upon us, the question of who we are cannot be separated from who he is.

The Name of Christ

I was preparing to go on a mission during President Ezra Taft Benson's presidency. In addition to encouraging all Church members to read the Book of Mormon every day, he said that he had a vision of missionaries going into the field having hundreds of verses of the Book of Mormon memorized. I took up the challenge and started writing out important Book of Mormon scriptures on 3x5 cards. I carried them around in my pocket, memorizing them between classes or when I was walking to or from BYU campus.

In the process of memorizing and pondering these scriptures, I changed. The Spirit helped me to understand the words I was studying, and I came to see things I had never seen before. These insights helped me have the courage to make changes in my life.

The scripture that had the deepest effect on me was from 2 Nephi 31. Through the language of this scripture, I began to understand that the baptismal covenant represented a profoundly different sense of myself and who I could become. I didn't learn the academic background of covenants as new relationships until after my mission, but the language and spirit of this verse brought the core truth into my heart.

In verse 13, Nephi thinks closely and seriously about the kind of life that is possible because of our covenant relationship with Christ and taking his name upon us.

> Wherefore, my beloved brethren, I know that if ye shall follow the Son, with full purpose of heart, acting no hypocrisy and no deception before God, but with real intent, repenting of your sins, witnessing unto the Father that ye are willing to take upon you the name of Christ, by baptism—yea, by following your Lord and your Savior down into the water, according to his word, behold, then shall ye receive the Holy Ghost; yea, then cometh the baptism of fire and of the Holy Ghost; and then can ye speak with the tongue of angels, and shout praises unto the Holy One of Israel. (2 Nephi 31:13)

Nephi isn't just saying we have to be really good. In saying that we must "follow the Son" into the waters of baptism and be "willing to take upon [us] the name of Christ," Nephi is saying that we need to take our covenants seriously. We need to really believe that we have taken Christ's name upon us.

His point about our needing to *want* to be in the covenant relationship is so important that he says it four different ways. We have to follow the Son (1) with full purpose of heart, (2) acting no hypocrisy and no deception, (3) with real intent, and (4) *willingly* taking the name of Christ upon ourselves. We have to really want to be like him.

When we make covenants, the actions of being baptized, receiving the endowment, and being sealed in the temple are the external ordinances we perform, but unless they are joined with our heart in making the covenants, the full effect of the new relationship is limited. Nephi is trying to help us understand that this new covenant relationship, enacted in the immersion of baptism ("following your Lord and your Savior down into the water, according to his word"), can bring us into an entirely new relationship with God. In this new relationship we are full of the Spirit—"then cometh the baptism of fire and of the Holy Ghost." It is not just being immersed in water or having the baptismal prayer recited that makes the relationship living. The ordinance and authority are necessary but not sufficient.

A relationship is real and alive when we live in that relationship. If we get married but then don't spend time together, we are not married the way we could or should be. If we adopt a child but then give her to someone else to raise, we are not living out the new relationship formed by the adoption.

Living out our covenant relationship starts by believing that we can be different and better people in and through Jesus Christ. It starts by believing that he has promised to help us become those people, people that have his character and attributes. This faith is what produces repentance. When we trust that we have access to the power of Christ in this new relationship, we can start to change and grow to become more like him. We can go forward, trusting that through our covenants he has given us his name and his power to do good and be good.

Covenant Identity

Covenants are there to give us confidence. This connection, as explained in Alma 7, jumped out at me during my mission in France. My missionary companion and I were standing in a long line at the post office, and I was passing the time by reading the Book of Mormon. I can still remember the excitement of seeing how faith not only precedes repentance and making covenants, but it also follows them. Alma spoke to the people of Gideon and explained baptism to them. He said, "Now I say unto you that ye must repent, and be born again; for the Spirit saith if ye are not born again ye cannot inherit the kingdom of heaven." So far it sounds like the basic, familiar pattern. But see what Alma explained can happen after they come and are baptized. He continued, "Therefore come and be baptized unto repentance, that ye may be washed from your sins, *that ye may have faith on the Lamb of God,* who taketh away the sins of the world, who is mighty to save and to cleanse from all unrighteousness" (Alma 7:14).

Part of the reason we are baptized is so we can have increased faith and confidence in the Lamb of God. He has taken away the sins of the world. He is mighty to save and to cleanse from all unrighteousness. Our covenant relationship allows us to have confidence that he has and will take away *our* sins and cleanse *us* from all unrighteousness.

We often turn this on its head and describe a covenant as a superpromise that we make but can never live up to. It is true that in all our covenants we promise to obey God, but that promise is part of a relationship in which Christ is giving us his name—if we are willing to receive it. Remember, names in the ancient world describe nature. Christ is promising to give us his nature. "We ask thee, Holy Father, that thy servants may go forth from this house armed with thy power, and that thy name may be upon them" (Doctrine and Covenants 109:22). At baptism we promise that we are willing to take his name upon us, and that is more fully realized in the temple endowment. Part of the dedicatory prayer of the Kirtland Temple was a plea that the gift of the Holy Ghost that we receive at baptism would be magnified and intensified: "[Grant] that they may grow up in thee, and receive a fulness of the Holy Ghost" (Doctrine and Covenants 109:15). As we receive his name more fully we can also receive his nature and his Spirit more fully. The Lord is promising to fill us with his Spirit and change our hearts so that we want to obey as he obeyed the Father.

We are reminded of this dimension of our covenant relationship most clearly in the sacrament prayers. We covenant weekly that we are "willing to take upon [us] the name of" Christ so that we "may always have his Spirit to be with [us]" (Doctrine and Covenants 20:77). Our willingness to live in this covenant relationship opens the door for him to pour out his Spirit. When we receive the Spirit, we have access to his enabling power. With this increased ability to live out this covenant relationship with him, we can become more and more like him.

But *we* have to want it. That is the absolute, foundational key to living in a covenant relationship. It is based entirely on our agency. The Lord wants to give us everything that he has and everything that he is. He wants us to be joint heirs with him of "all that [the] Father hath" (Doctrine and Covenants 84:38). He wants to give us desires to do good and hate evil. He wants to give us forgiveness when we are weak and power to become strong.

We must believe in the reality of those covenant promises. To trust these promises we must believe in the reality of the covenant relationships that we make in The Church of Jesus Christ of Latter-day Saints. We need a testimony of God the Father, his Son Jesus Christ, and of the restoration, through the Prophet Joseph Smith, of priesthood keys that continue to be held by the current President of the Church. Without this witness, we will not have confidence in the words that were said by a priesthood holder when we were baptized: "Having been commissioned of Jesus Christ, I baptize you in the name of the Father, and of the Son, and of the Holy Ghost" (Doctrine and Covenants 20:73). Without this witness, we will not have confidence that we can accept the gift that was offered in our confirmation when we were told by an authorized Melchizedek Priesthood holder, "Receive the Holy Ghost." Without faith, there will be no repentance. Without faith in Christ, we will not live the covenant life that is being offered us in this new relationship.

Often we feel so trapped in our own weakness that we think we can never live up to what we have promised. Our experience with our own fears, inclinations, and weaknesses leaves us feeling imprisoned. Sometimes we have done things that we regret. Sometimes our lack of desire to do good leads to letting opportunities pass us by, leaving us with guilt and regret. We become more hopeless about our ability to change or live up to what we have promised. We think, "I'm not strong enough. I'm not celestial material. This is just the way I am." Our sense of self in itself can be the bondage that binds us down and keeps us from moving forward and becoming what we have been promised we can become.

Even when we are weak, the Lord is strong. We must remember that we are not alone and not abandoned. Having hope in our own ability to live up to the lofty promises and expectations of our covenant relationship is based on faith in ourselves. But faith in ourselves will never get us out of the depth of our captivity. Hope in a gospel sense is not tied to confidence in our own strength, but to better understanding the nature of our covenant relationship and who we have covenanted with. When we understand and begin to trust the One who has made covenant promises, then we will look to him for help.

We have promised so much. But what we often fail to appreciate is that in these new relationships we are promised far more by the Lord. Just as the ancient concept of covenants as relationships opens up a new way to think about who we are and who we can become, the world of the ancient Israelites offers additional clues as to how the Lord will help us get there when we so often feel trapped by weakness and sin. The concept of redemption becomes clearer when we understand who the Lord is and what his covenant relationship with us means.

CHAPTER 3

REDEMPTION
gā'al

My earliest memories of spiritual impressions come from times I was singing hymns, praying, or bearing my testimony. As I grew older and had additional opportunities to serve, I came to find additional personal revelation when preparing to give a talk, teach a lesson, or help someone with their questions. I first understood the witness in Alma 7 about Christ having taken upon himself our sins and sicknesses in just this way during my first year at BYU as a transfer student. I was living on campus in May Hall, and in conversation, a young woman down the hall had expressed her confusion about why Christ, a perfect and blameless person, had suffered. As I found and shared verses about Christ taking upon himself our pains and sicknesses, they came alive for me and I understood more of the breadth of Christ's Atonement.

Another memorable learning moment came when I was preparing a sacrament meeting talk the year after my mission. I was living in the Italian house near BYU campus, and I remembered a cupboard that had

As our Redeemer, Christ brings us out of bondage and allows us to begin a new life.

some tan-colored crepe paper used for decorations at parties. I wrapped it around my arm under my flowered dress and went to our sacrament meeting in the lobby of the engineering building. As I started my talk, I rolled up my sleeve. The crepe paper looked just like a wrapped bandage, and everyone stared. I asked the congregation if they would stop to ask if someone else had hurt me or if I had hurt myself before helping me if I came to them bleeding. I asked if they would limit giving care and healing only to people who deserved it. As I spoke, we all felt a witness of the mercy, love, and healing power of the Lord as we came to understand more fully that his redemption is offered to all.

Studying the scholarly literature on redemption in the Old Testament and the ancient Near East during my senior year, I realized that within the vocabulary of redemption was a very powerful idea. Very simply, to be redeemed is to be bought out of bondage. Even the English word carries this root concept of buying back. For example, bottles and cans are redeemed when they are returned in exchange for a payment. A similar term is *to ransom*. At its core, *redemption* occurs when someone in captivity is released through the payment of a price.

Redemption from slavery was a widespread practice in the ancient world. People became slaves because they were captured in war and then sold by their captors. Even more tragically, people also became slaves by selling themselves into bondage or by being sold by a family member because there was no other way to pay off a debt. However a person got into bondage, another person could act as a redeemer and pay the price to free them from bondage and slavery. Redemption wasn't for the worthy who had their lives together. Redemption was for those who were enslaved.

Christ is our Savior. Christ is our Redeemer. It is easy for us to blur distinctions between words that are so similar in many ways. The effect for us is the same—we were in trouble, and thanks to him, we are safe, we are saved, we are out of trouble. But, while saving is a good general-purpose word, it doesn't give any details about how the action was completed. For example, if someone is pulled from a flood or a burning building, they are saved. They needed help and someone stepped in to help them. So we can rightly say, with deep gratitude, that Jesus Christ is our Savior and the Savior of the world.

The Old Testament concept of redemption offers us additional nuance and specificity about salvation. Redemption is a subset of salvation. The term *redeem* focuses on how we are saved and what we are being saved from. *Redemption* emphasizes that we are saved from slavery through the payment of a price. To say that Christ is our Redeemer emphasizes that he paid to buy us out of bondage. The gospel message behind this is taught very eloquently by Peter when he explained that "ye were not redeemed with corruptible things, as silver and gold, from your vain conversation [or conduct] received by tradition from your fathers; but with the precious blood of Christ, as of a lamb without blemish and without spot" (1 Peter 1:18–19). The Book of Mormon joins the New Testament in pointing to the spiritual meaning of *redemption* and the witness that Jesus Christ is Jehovah, the Redeemer of Israel.

The Redeemer of Israel

One place where the message of the Lord's role as the Redeemer is taught most clearly is in the record of Abinadi's short ministry. "I would that ye should understand that God himself shall come down among the children of men, and shall redeem his people" (Mosiah 15:1). The immensity of the witness that Abinadi gave dawned on me one Sunday evening in December the year before my mission. I was bundled up and walking to the Provo Tabernacle to attend the Adventsingen, an evening of Christmas music and scripture. As I walked, I sang to myself the Christmas carol "Once in David's Royal City." While singing the second verse, I received a witness of the love and condescension manifest in the coming of Jehovah to earth to save us.

> He came down to earth from heaven,
> Who is God and Lord of all,
> And his shelter was a stable,
> And his cradle was a stall;
> With the poor, and mean, and lowly,
> Lived on earth our Savior holy.[1]

His humility to become mortal and vulnerable became very real to me at that moment. When we recognize our need for a Redeemer, we are humbled by his humility to come down to earth in a human body to feel our pains and to suffer for us.

Abinadi taught the priests of King Noah that it was through the ransom price of the Lord Jehovah's own suffering that we have the opportunity for redemption. The priests, however, were confident that their own obedience was the source of their salvation. Abinadi first reminded them of their failure to keep the commandments of the law of Moses, underlining their need for a redeemer. He then shared the Messianic prophecy of Isaiah 53, which points to the sacrifice of Christ, the one who would be "wounded for our transgressions" and "bruised for our iniquities," "brought as a lamb to the slaughter" as the Lord "laid on him the iniquities of us all" (53:5–7). This is how the Lord redeemed his people. "For were it not for the redemption which he hath made for his people, which was prepared from the foundation of the world, I say unto you, were it not for this, all mankind must have perished" (Mosiah 15:19). This witness of Jesus Christ as Jehovah, the Redeemer of Israel, runs throughout the Book of Mormon, but because of our unfamiliarity with the ancient concepts behind redemption it is easy to miss the witness that we are receiving in the Book of Mormon as well as in the Bible.

To more fully appreciate the witness of all these books of scripture, we have to return to ancient words. In ancient Israel the action of redeeming from bondage could be expressed with two different Hebrew verbs. The first, *pādāh*, is related to words for *redeem* in other Semitic languages. It reflects the general practice of redeeming that was widespread in the ancient Near East. But there is a verb that is found only in Hebrew: *gā 'al*. The person who acts to redeem in this sense is a *gō 'ēl*. The best translation of *gō 'ēl* is "kinsman-redeemer." The kind of redemption that is described by *gā 'al* and done by the *gō 'ēl* is not generic. It could not be done by anyone for anyone. It is based on familial relationship. The *gō 'ēl* was the oldest male member of an extended family who had the familial obligation to restore that which had become unbalanced. The *gō 'ēl* redeemed family members who had become enslaved for whatever reason. Maybe they had been captured. Maybe they had sold themselves or had been sold into slavery. The *gō 'ēl* was there to make things right and to bring family members back to their rightful place.

The Lord Jehovah is known throughout the Old Testament as the *gō 'ēl*, the Redeemer of Israel. The children of Israel knew that they could count on him to deliver them and bring them out of bondage. They knew that he wasn't just any god, he was Jehovah, their God, the Father of their salvation. They knew that his redemption grew out of the family relationship formed through the covenants they had made. "Doubtless thou art our father, though Abraham be ignorant of us, and Israel acknowledge us not: thou, O Lord, art our father, our redeemer; thy name is from everlasting" (Isaiah 63:16). The covenant relationship with the Lord as their spiritual father was stronger than even their sense of descent from their famed ancestors, Abraham and Jacob/Israel. They knew their *gō 'ēl*, the Kinsman-Redeemer of Israel, would never forget them.

In the book of Deuteronomy, the Israelites were reminded that the Lord's role as Redeemer (*gō'ēl*) extended from the covenants that he made with Abraham, Isaac, and Jacob/Israel. The descendants of Israel had been in captivity in Egypt for hundreds of years and had forgotten the Lord, but he had not forgotten them. The children of Israel are told that *"because he would keep the oath which he had sworn unto your fathers,* hath the Lord brought you out with a mighty hand, and *redeemed you out of the house of bondmen,* from the hand of Pharaoh king of Egypt" (Deuteronomy 7:8; emphasis added). The Lord remembers his people. He remembers his covenant promises and covenant relationship.

The Lord's covenants with Abraham, Isaac, and Jacob are the foundation of the story of the house of Israel. But the covenants with the patriarchs are not the only covenants in the Old Testament. After the children of Israel were redeemed from Egypt, they collectively made a covenant with Jehovah at Mount Sinai. We know this covenant especially well because it is associated with the law of Moses and the Ten Commandments.

A large portion of the books of Exodus, Leviticus, Numbers, and Deuteronomy is dedicated to laying out and explaining the relationship of the Lord and Israel that is expressed in the law of Moses. The demands of this covenant relationship were elaborate. Many of these chapters are so nuanced and detailed that we can't even get through them. They detail obligations that were critical for their covenant relationship but that are foreign to us. This is where it can help to really step back and think about the big picture. We know from modern-day revelation that through Moses, the Lord had invited Israel to enter into the Melchizedek Priesthood covenants of the patriarchs, but they refused his invitation. He did still enter into a covenant with all the house of Israel, but it was a lesser, Levitical Priesthood covenant (see Doctrine and Covenants 84:19–26).

But, even with a lesser covenant, the children of Israel were still the Lord's covenant people. They also received blessings from the covenants made earlier with their fathers. In Exodus 6:4–8 the Lord reminded them that it was because of his covenant relationship with the patriarchs that he delivered them out of bondage. He started with the covenant basis for his act of redemption: "*And I have also established my covenant with them* [the patriarchs], *to give them the land of Canaan, the land of their pilgrimage, wherein they were strangers.*" The promises associated with this covenant also extended to the descendants of the patriarchs. The Lord continued, "And I have also heard the groaning of the children of Israel, whom the Egyptians keep in bondage; and *I have remembered my covenant*. Wherefore say unto the children of Israel, I am the Lord, and I will bring you out from under the burdens of the Egyptians, and I will rid you out of their bondage, and *I will redeem you with a stretched out arm, and with great judgments.*" The covenant was the basis for his role as the Redeemer of Israel.

The Lord then promised that he would allow all the people of Israel to covenant with him. "*And I will take you to me for a people, and I will be to you a God*: and ye shall know that I am the Lord your God, which bringeth you out from under the burdens of the Egyptians. And I will bring you in unto the land, concerning the which I did swear to give it to Abraham, to Isaac, and to Jacob; and I will give it you for an heritage: I am the Lord" (Exodus 6:4–8; emphasis added). The Lord's faithfulness to act as Israel's Kinsman-Redeemer was because of his earlier covenant relationship with the patriarchs.

The children of Israel were in bondage. They were Egyptian slaves. They were not doing anything that made them special or worthy. We have every reason to think that they were living, thinking, and worshipping like the Egyptians in whose land they had dwelt for centuries. But the Lord remembered his covenant relationship. He remembered his covenant promises to the patriarchs. He was faithful and delivered the Israelites out of captivity. Once they were delivered, he offered them the opportunity to covenant with him themselves.

While they didn't have the faith to enter into the full Melchizedek Priesthood covenants of the patriarchs (see Doctrine and Covenants 84:23–26), the Lord's faithfulness to earlier covenant relationships gave the children of Israel confidence to enter into a covenant relationship with him—the law of Moses. They saw that he fulfilled the promises he had made, and they had confidence he would fulfill his promises in this new relationship with them.

Looking to the Redeemer

The understanding of the Lord Jehovah as the Redeemer of Israel not only pervades the Old Testament, but it is a foundational concept for Lehi and his family in the Book of Mormon. The Book of Mormon record makes it clear that redemption was associated with the future coming of the Redeemer. Lehi's initial revelation and preaching were rejected because he, like the other prophets, told the inhabitants of Jerusalem that they needed to repent and that they needed redemption. He "manifested plainly of the coming of a Messiah, and also the redemption of the world" and they responded by being "angry with him; yea, even as with the prophets of old, whom they had cast out, and stoned, and slain; and they also sought his life, that they might take it away" (1 Nephi 1:19–20). The message that we need redeeming can often be taken as an insult rather than as a message of hope.

We can see how Lehi's witness of the Redeemer was consistent, even when it was not well received. Lehi's first prophecies to his family also focused on the coming of a Redeemer. Lehi "spake concerning the prophets, how great a number had testified of these things, concerning this Messiah, of whom he had spoken, or this Redeemer of the world. Wherefore, all mankind were in a lost and in a fallen state, and ever would be save they should rely on this Redeemer" (1 Nephi 10:5–6). Lehi had a clear vision of the Redeemer as the hope of Israel and of the world.

Redemption was also an important concept for Nephi from our earliest encounters with him. Nephi recounted the biblical story of the redemption of Israel to help his brothers increase their faith. He wanted them to have confidence that the Lord was their Redeemer. He wanted them to trust that the Redeemer of Israel would help them in their challenge to get the plates. "Let us go up again unto Jerusalem, and let us be faithful in keeping the commandments of the Lord; for behold he is mightier than all the earth, then why not mightier than Laban and his fifty, yea, or even than his tens of thousands?" (1 Nephi 4:1).

Having been chased out by Laban, the brothers were experiencing their own kind of bondage. They despaired and felt powerless to keep the command to obtain the plates, but Nephi encouraged them to remember the power of the Lord. He knew they needed greater trust in the Lord to have the courage to be faithful to his commandments. "Therefore let us go up; let us be strong like unto Moses; for he truly spake unto the waters of the Red Sea and they divided hither and thither, and our fathers came through, out of captivity, on dry ground, and the armies of Pharaoh did follow and were drowned in the waters of the Red Sea" (1 Nephi 4:2). Nephi believed that they had the same claim on the Lord's help as did the ancient Israelites, and so he was full of faith that there would also be divine intervention in their own time of helplessness. "Let us go up; the Lord is able to deliver us, even as our fathers, and to destroy Laban, even as the Egyptians" (1 Nephi 4:3).

Over and over again, Nephi referred back to the account of the redemption of Israel from bondage in Egypt to give hope and courage to his brothers who were struggling. When they did not want to work at building a ship, Nephi drew these connections to the ancient Israelites at the time of Moses to help them see the need for action. "Do ye believe that our fathers, who were the children of Israel, would have been led away out of the hands of the Egyptians if they had not hearkened unto the words of the Lord?" (1 Nephi 17:23). Nephi wanted them to see the connection between faith in the Redeemer and obedience to his commands.

Nephi particularly focused on the idea that the ancient Israelites had to participate in their redemption. If they hadn't had the faith to listen to the words of the Lord through Moses, they would not have been led out of the hands of the Egyptians. Nephi reminded Laman and Lemuel "that the children of Israel were in bondage; and ye know that they were laden with tasks, which were grievous to be borne" (1 Nephi 17:25). Nephi recounted again how the Lord brought them out of bondage, divided the waters of the Red Sea, drowned the armies of Pharaoh, fed them with manna, and brought water out of the rock for them. Nephi was likely reminding Laman and Lemuel of the help they had received thus far on their journey from Jerusalem, but he also emphasized that the ancient Israelites had turned from their relationship with their Redeemer, even though he had delivered them and been so attentive to their needs. "And notwithstanding they being led, the Lord their God, their Redeemer, going before them, leading them by day and giving light unto them by night, and doing all things for them which were expedient for man to receive, they hardened their hearts and blinded their minds, and reviled against Moses and against the true and living God" (1 Nephi 17:30). Relationships have two sides, and these stories warn us that we must live in those relationships for them to be alive for us.

Nephi's relationship with the Lord Jehovah had become increasingly personal through the years as he continued to exercise faith and to have his own revelatory experiences. Nephi not only learned that Jehovah was the Redeemer of Israel and took courage from accounts of previous redemptive acts, but he also saw this redeeming power in his own life as he was faithful to his covenant relationship.

Nephi clearly understood that Israel's covenant relationship with the Lord was what made him their Kinsman-Redeemer. Nephi explained this concept to Laman and Lemuel, saying, "And he loveth those who will have him to be their God. Behold, he loved our fathers, and he covenanted with them, yea, even Abraham, Isaac, and Jacob; and he remembered the covenants which he had made; wherefore, he did bring them [the Israelites] out of the land of Egypt" (1 Nephi 17:40). Covenants create a new family relationship. In ancient Israel redemption was the responsibility of the Kinsman-Redeemer. The Lord Jehovah was the Redeemer of Israel because of the covenants he had made with the patriarchs, and he brought the children of Israel out of bondage. Like Nephi, we can come to appreciate how the Lord is also our personal Redeemer because of the covenants we have made. As we grow to love and trust him, we will look to him for our own redemption.

Our Redemption

But even though we look to him for our redemption and promise to obey him, we still get into trouble. We are stuck and are sometimes even in bondage, just like the Israelites. Even after their initial deliverance, the Israelites had many opportunities to look to the Lord as their Kinsman-Redeemer throughout their history. There were many times that they were lost, threatened, or in captivity. A poignant expression of looking to the Lord as Kinsman-Redeemer in times of help is found in Psalm 74:1–2. Here the Psalmist cries out: "O God, why hast thou cast us off for ever? why doth thine anger smoke against the sheep of thy pasture? Remember thy congregation, which thou hast purchased of old; the rod of thine inheritance, which thou hast redeemed." This plea reflects the desperate feeling of being in bondage—feeling cast off from the Lord's presence. But it also recalls and relies on the memory of the Lord's redemption of and covenant relationship with Israel.

Remembering that we *have* been redeemed in the past increases our confidence that we *will* be redeemed from present and future troubles. Our bondage will usually not be external, but will rather be captivity to the natural man in us. Satan wants us to believe that our weaknesses are our true nature and that we can't leave this condition of spiritual bondage. Knowing that the Lord is our Kinsman-Redeemer gives us confidence to ask for help, even when we are the ones that have sold ourselves into bondage. "For thus saith the Lord: Ye have sold yourselves for naught, and ye shall be redeemed without money" (3 Nephi 20:38; Isaiah 52:3). Even Nephi, who had lived a life of covenant faithfulness, struggled with his own weaknesses and failures. Even he needed to remember that he had been redeemed from the natural man in him and could be redeemed again when he failed to live up to expectations.

In the psalm of Nephi we see Nephi wresting with his feeling of failure and helplessness to do and be what he knew that he should: "O wretched man that I am! Yea, my heart sorroweth because of my flesh; my soul grieveth because of mine iniquities. I am encompassed about, because of the temptations and the sins which do so easily beset me. And when I desire to rejoice, my heart groaneth because of my sins" (2 Nephi 4:17–19). Nephi understood covenants and lived out his covenants. But he was also human and weak. He didn't always live up to every promise that he made and every loving, noble impulse that he felt. He sometimes gave way to other feelings, which he then regretted. He could have sunk down into despair when he looked at the things he had done wrong or left undone. He experienced the feeling of being captive to the "temptations and the sins which do so easily beset me," but Nephi knew that because of his covenant relationship with the Lord, he wasn't dependent on his own strength alone.

The turning point in the psalm of Nephi is Nephi's looking up from feeling imprisoned by his sinful state to trust in the freedom offered by his Redeemer. Nephi did not hide from himself—or from us—the experience of being trapped by his past choices and his own weakness. "And when I desire to rejoice, my heart groaneth because of my sins; nevertheless, I know in whom I have trusted" (2 Nephi 4:19). "I know in whom I have trusted." Nephi had exercised faith in his Redeemer previously, and he exercised that faith again. By remembering the redeeming love and power of the Lord, Nephi was freed from the bondage of his own despair and regained hope that he could do and be more than he could by himself. "My God hath been my support; he hath led me through mine afflictions in the wilderness; and he hath preserved me upon the waters of the great deep. He hath filled me with his love, even unto the consuming of my flesh. He hath confounded mine enemies, unto the causing of them to quake before me" (2 Nephi 4:20–22).

Nephi knew that his prayers for deliverance had been heard in the past, and he knew that they would continue to be heard. The Lord remembers his people. Because he remembered his relationship with the Lord, Nephi had courage to walk away from the captivity of despairing that he could never be what he needed to be. "Awake, my soul! No longer droop in sin. Rejoice, O my heart, and give place no more for the enemy of my soul" (2 Nephi 4:28). Nephi realized that he needed to wake up to the reality of the Redeemer that was bigger than his own weakness. He realized that the Lord's power and grace transcended his own mistakes and personal struggles. He chose to focus on gratitude for redeeming love and redeeming power rather than to despair at his own past or at his own weak nature. "Rejoice, O my heart, and cry unto the Lord, and say: O Lord, I will praise thee forever; yea, my soul will rejoice in thee, my God, and the rock of my salvation" (2 Nephi 4:30).

It is critical that we see this internal shift in Nephi from the captivity of despair to the hope and joy of redemption as a result of faith in the Redeemer. Nephi didn't cheer himself up by telling himself that what he had done (or left undone) didn't matter. He didn't try to convince himself that he was better than he thought he was. This account is not about positive self-image or positive thinking. It is a brutally honest struggle to abandon the despair over our own spiritual captivity to the natural man by beginning to exercise faith in the Redeemer. We can actually see Nephi's prayer for redemption in the text: "O Lord, wilt thou redeem my soul? Wilt thou deliver me out of the hands of mine enemies? Wilt thou make me that I may shake at the appearance of sin?" (2 Nephi 4:31). Nephi knew that he didn't just need redeeming from what he had done, but from who he was. Christ has come to bring us out of the bondage of guilt from past choices and also from the bondage of a fallen nature that will keep us repeating sinful choices. Nephi recognized the power of the natural man part of himself, that part of our fallen nature that can keep pulling us back into spiritual bondage, and called out for redeeming help to have a change of heart so that he "may shake at the appearance of sin."

Trusting Our Redeemer

Looking to our covenant relationship with the Lord by calling out for him to redeem us can provide peace and hope in our darkest times. These dark times may come when things are not working out in our circumstances. They may come when we are filled with regret. They also come when we are struggling to be more and to be better. The covenant promises give us confidence that the fires we go through will have a sanctifying power. Because of our covenant relationship with the One who can cause all things to work together for our good, we can experience reality differently (see Romans 8:28). As we come to know "the greatness of God" we can trust that "he shall consecrate [our] afflictions for [our] gain" (2 Nephi 2:2).

This divine promise of redemption is expressed in the powerful text of the hymn "How Firm a Foundation." In the scripture behind this text, Isaiah 43:1–3, we can see how the redemption and covenant relationship of Israel serve as a source of comfort for present fears: "But now thus saith the Lord that created thee, O Jacob, and he that formed thee, O Israel, *Fear not: for I have redeemed thee, I have called thee by thy name; thou art mine.* When thou passest through the waters, I will be with thee; and through the rivers, they shall not overflow thee: when thou walkest through the fire, thou shalt not be burned; neither shall the flame kindle upon thee. For I am the Lord thy God, the Holy One of Israel, thy Saviour" (Isaiah 43:1–3; emphasis added). Here again the redemption of Israel is connected with covenant relationship. We see both the giving of a name and the sense of belonging between the Lord and Israel: "I have called thee by thy name; thou art mine" (Isaiah 43:1). When we fear the water of our trials will overflow us and that we will be burned by the fire of our experiences, we can look to these promises. We can trust in this relationship.

Remembering that the covenant relationship itself is the source of our confidence can help us have hope no matter where we are on the covenant path. Our confidence does not need to be that we have never made mistakes. Our confidence does not need to be in our flawless character or perfectly reliable nature. If we tried to base our confidence in our own perfection then we would be lying to God and ourselves. Christ makes covenants with us so we know that we can put our trust in him even when we are at our weakest. He is there for us when we have completely blown it.

We don't need to get ourselves out of trouble and cleaned up in order to ask for help. We can be flawed and weak and stuck. We can admit to ourselves that that we are "encompassed about, because of the temptations and the sins which do so easily beset [us]" (2 Nephi 4:18). We can acknowledge that we are bound down by habits and desires that are trapping and limiting us because that is what redemption is for. We can ask for and receive redemption no matter what our problems are.

In fact, until we can admit that we are in bondage to the natural man in us, we will never know how much we need a Redeemer. As long as our confidence is in ourselves, we will actually find the idea of needing redemption an insult. This is exactly what happened in John 8 when the Lord told those who believed on him that "if ye continue in my word, then are ye my disciples indeed; and ye shall know the truth, and the truth shall make you free" (John 8:31–32). These believers took the idea that they needed freeing as a slight to their good name and impeccable character. "We are not the slaves of any man!" they responded. "We don't need to be made free." By refusing to see that they were in spiritual bondage and needed a Redeemer, they missed the opportunity to receive the freedom they were being offered.

I know how tempting it is to think of oneself as good and to think that the Atonement is for other people, the people who have made poor choices and who haven't had the discipline to live worthy lives. If we pay our tithing, keep the Word of Wisdom, go to church on Sunday, and generally try keep the commandments, it's easy to fall into the self-perception of the Pharisee who prayed to God, thanking him that he was "not as other men are" (Luke 18:11). But in that parable, it was the publican whom Christ praised. It was the publican who could not lift up his eyes to heaven but prayed that God would be merciful to him—a sinner—who went away justified and not the self-righteous Pharisee.

For me it was not until I took President Benson's challenge to read the Book of Mormon every day that I had the courage to see myself as a sinner, one who needed a Redeemer. Before that it was easy to see the bad things that I avoided and the good things that I did. I patted myself on the back, thanking God that I was "not as other men are." The irony is that the witness of redemption that runs through the Book of Mormon comes with an equally clear witness of our lost and fallen state as human beings. It's not a pretty picture when we start to look more closely at why we do what we do and find pride, selfishness, and fear mingled in with outwardly praiseworthy lives. It's not a pretty picture when we start to look at the good things we have left undone out of fear or lack of love. The more we see, the more tempted we are to despair and feel that we are stuck, that we can't change. But that lie about our state is just as hurtful as the lie that we are fine and don't need to change. Neither is true because both deny the reality of Christ's redemption.

In the American folk hymn "What Wondrous Love Is This," one verse describes how it feels to exercise faith in redemption. "When I was sinking down beneath God's righteous frown, Christ laid aside His crown for my soul."[2] Getting a witness of the redemption of Christ must come as we are "sinking down beneath God's righteous frown." We have to be willing to admit that we are in bondage to know that we need redemption. At the same time, until we trust that we have a Redeemer, it is almost impossible to break through the self-deceptions that comfort us into thinking either that what we are doing isn't a problem or that it's just the way we are and so there is nothing that we can do about it. We have to face the justice of God and "acknowledge . . . that all his judgments are just" (Alma 12:15) and that we really have "sold [ourselves] for naught" (3 Nephi 20:38) in order to embrace the gift of Christ's redeeming power. We must admit we are in captivity before we can look to our Redeemer for help.

The Song of Redeeming Love

When we feel hope that we can be forgiven and change, then we begin to feel those chains fall. This freedom causes us to sing the "song of redeeming love." Alma asked the people in Zarahemla that if they had "felt to sing the song of redeeming love, . . . [could they] feel so now?" (Alma 5:26). Staying in a relationship with Christ where we don't just *know* in the abstract that he is our Redeemer but instead actually *feel* to sing the song of redeeming love requires being redeemed on a regular basis.

This is not to advocate that we fall back into the same patterns of behavior that Christ ransomed us from. Far from it. That would be hoping to be redeemed in our sins rather than being redeemed from them (see Helaman 5:10). Christ gave himself as a ransom so that we could walk in a life of freedom from sin. But the process of recognizing and repenting of being fallen and ungodly people is not a onetime experience. It is a lifelong experience.

While sanctification requires daily repentance, we keep repenting of different kinds of things as we move closer to Christ. Living a life of faith and daily repentance is living out our covenant relationship with Christ. He doesn't need us to pretend that we are perfect and that we don't need redeeming anymore. He has power to fully bring us out of the captivity and power of Satan, and he will give us power to stay out of the chains of the evil one and to "walk in newness of life" (Romans 6:4). As we come to know him more fully through our covenant relationship, we come to know the Truth—our Redeemer—that makes us free.

This is the truth that that can give us power to fight off the temptation to think that we can never change, that this is just the way we are. The redemption of Christ is the ultimate truth that can break any chain that would bind us down to destruction. The covenants that we make with him are our source of confidence that we are never permanently stuck or in bondage. With Nephi, we can "know in whom [we] have trusted" and fight off the feeling that we are permanently trapped by whatever kinds of chains and weaknesses are keeping us from living lives of holiness.

Christ's witness to us is that he has paid the price of our redemption. If we are still in bondage, it is not because the door of the prison is still locked. Even when we still feel the dark chill of that prison, we must exercise faith in the redemption of him who created us and step out of the chains and into the light. Each act of humble obedience and contrite repentance is an exercise of faith in Christ's redemption. He has provided the means by which we can exercise faith unto redemption. We can look to him and live.

Once we feel our burden of guilt and regret lifted and we begin to walk free from the sense of ourselves as forever trapped by our past and our own weakness, what is next? What does the Lord expect of us when we have left our own bondage, our own "Egypt"? The account of the Israelites again points the way.

When Moses was called to lead the children of Israel out of bondage, the Lord explained, "Certainly I will be with thee; and this shall be a token unto thee, that I have sent thee: When thou hast brought forth the people out of Egypt, ye shall serve God upon this mountain" (Exodus 3:12). As slaves in Egypt, Israel was serving an Egyptian master; however, after Jehovah freed them from bondage, they were to serve him as their new master. Living to serve God becomes an expression of our gratitude and a form of worship.

Notes

1. Cecil F. Alexander, "Once in Royal David's City," in *Hymns* (Salt Lake City: The Church of Jesus Christ of Latter-day Saints, 1985), no. 205.
2. "What Wondrous Love Is This," in *The Hymnal 1982 Companion*, vol 3b, ed. Raymond F. Glover (New York: Church Hymnal, 1990), 826–27.

CHAPTER 4

WORSHIP

ḥwh and *ʿābad*

How do we live once the Truth has set us free? What is life as a redeemed person supposed to feel like or look like? Driving up to Idaho to visit my husband's family one summer vacation, we stopped for a delicious lunch at a drive-in near Brigham City. We listened to the radio as we ate. A caller expressed his relief in leaving the Church. Now, he declared, nobody would tell him what to do with his money, what to do with his time, and what to wear. He was free. For me, this highlighted the life of worship that we are invited into as disciples in Christ's Church. We are told what we should do with 10 percent of our increase, what we should do with our time on the Sabbath, and what we should wear to keep our temple covenants. We are bound.

Freedom has modern connotations that bring to mind self-rule and self-will. The ideal is doing what we want, how we want, when we want. Any constraints or limits to our autonomy are seen as putting us in bondage. But when we look at the redemption that Jehovah offered Israel, we

FINDING CHRIST IN THE COVENANT PATH

In this new relationship, we leave the world behind and worship as we bow down and serve him.

see that it was not to be freed from serving the Egyptians in order to run free in a modern sense. Because of our redemption, we belong to Christ and publicly acknowledge our submission to our Lord and Redeemer and his living prophets through a life of obedience. It may seem counterintuitive that the freedom God offers us can be described in the same terms as the bondage we're being freed from. Unlike slavery in human history, which debases the value of human life, becoming the servants of the Lord is being like Christ, who did the will of the Father in all things. Our submission is what makes us Saints. Our willingness to live his way is how we worship.

Our Lord

From the Old Testament we learn of the relationship between the redemption of the children of Israel and their responsibility to serve and worship their true Lord. This connection is repeated in what Moses is told: "And thou shalt say unto Pharaoh, Thus saith the Lord, Israel is my son, even my firstborn: and I say unto thee, Let my son go, *that he may serve me*" (Exodus 4:22–23; emphasis added). We are brought from the captivity of serving sin to the freedom of serving the Lord.

WORSHIP

The Old Testament helps us understand why we should want to see ourselves as God's servants, those who are grateful to bow down and serve only him. In the Ten Commandments, part of the covenant with the house of Israel, the Lord told the Israelites, "I am the Lord thy God, which have brought thee out of the land of Egypt, out of the house of bondage. Thou shalt have no other gods before me" (Exodus 20:2–3). The Lord's position as *our* Lord derives from his having brought us out from the bondage of another lord, from being the servants of sin (see John 8:34). Because of the redemption, the Israelites became God's *ʿăbādîm*, his servants or slaves.

This type of service, or slavery, is markedly different from human bondage. In Leviticus 25, in a discussion of slavery under the law of Moses, the Lord explains that Israelites who become slaves have a different status than foreign slaves. "For they are my servants, which I brought forth out of the land of Egypt: they shall not be sold as bondmen" (Leviticus 25:42). This chapter explains that fellow Israelites cannot be human property, as can a foreign slave, because of the redemption. This sense of belonging to the Lord as his servants or slaves because of the redemption from bondage in Egypt is a foreshadowing of the spiritual principle taught by Paul: "ye are not your own[;] for ye are bought with a price" (1 Corinthians 6:19–20).

The language of being servants or slaves of God is widespread in both the Old and New Testaments, but these texts also originate from cultures in which slavery was widespread. This is another ancient concept that pushes us to dig deep into ancient language and thought to see what we can understand and experience in our present world. Let's start with some key words to work ourselves into this way of seeing ourselves and our relationship with God.

In the vocabulary of the Old Testament, the Hebrew verbs meaning "bow down" (*ḥwh* or *ḥwy*) and "serve" (*ʿābad*) are both often translated as "worship." These verbs describe the physical expression of a relationship of submission to authority—to bow down and to serve. We acknowledge another as our lord by bowing down and serving. The way we behave is an embodiment of this relationship. The respect and obedience embodied in bowing down and serving shows our relationship to the one who has authority to command, the one to whom we owe worship.

We can see this elaborated in the Ten Commandments. An explanation given after the first commandment to worship only the Lord clarifies, "Thou shalt not *bow* thyself to them, nor *serve* them: for I the Lord thy God am a jealous God" (Exodus 20:5; emphasis added). Because of their covenant relationship, the Israelites were to worship only Jehovah. He was their master and they were to serve only him. Likewise, the physical prostration of bowing down was due only to him. The act of bowing down was an expression of humility that recognized one's dependence on and submission to another.

Now, of course, dependence and submission are also words that can make us flinch in a modern context, but let's keep thinking about how bowing down and serving in the biblical world were ways of worshipping. One thing that can help us navigate this ancient culture is to see serving God in terms of our own redemption. Being God's servant can become more understandable when we think of the immensity of the ransom that was paid for our souls. When we feel a gratitude so deep that we would do anything for the One who paid the price for our escape from bondage, we can start to understand worship as bowing down and serving. Paul again brings out the spiritual dimension of this relationship: "But God be thanked, that ye were the servants of sin, but ye have obeyed from the heart that form of doctrine which was delivered you. Being then made free from sin, ye became the servants of righteousness" (Romans 6:17–18).

The need to keep our obedience rooted in a recognition of our debt to Christ is likely why we promise to "always remember him" in the sacrament prayer on the bread before we promise to "keep his commandments which he has given [us]" (Doctrine and Covenants 20:77). When we always remember Christ and what he has done for us, keeping his commandments becomes an expression of our gratitude and love. Our obedience is an outward sign of our redemption from the bondage of sin.

The serious obligations of obedience that we take upon ourselves in our covenant relationship acknowledge that we have committed to do his will in all things. We are not our own. We have been bought with a price. Our choice to obey his will in all things is a choice to bow down before his authority. Our choice to obey is a choice to worship with our lives.

Bowing Down

Again, in the modern world freedom and autonomy are elevated to almost unquestionable status. Bowing down just seems wrong. The idea of owing obedience or homage to anyone, let alone belonging to anyone, can make us extremely nervous. The endless abuse of power throughout history makes us grateful to live in a time and part of the world in which power is limited by law. We don't have to do things because others tell us to unless they are legally authorized to do so. Kings and nobles once had the right to rule and command simply by birth. The idea that others have the right to our obedience flies in the face of a Western, post-Enlightenment worldview.

The democratic urge to feel that we are our own boss can make it difficult to be in any relationships in which others tell us what to do. Even employers and parents struggle to set guidelines and expectations. Assumptions that no one has the right to command us will not help us navigate a divine relationship that precedes and transcends time and history. We must go back to ancient concepts, but we must also recognize that we are agents in this relationship: we chose Christ as our Lord and our King. We are not born as subjects to a sovereign whose will is law merely because of geography.

When we choose to be part of the kingdom of God by making covenants, we choose Christ as our King. We choose a relationship in which we promise to do his will. In this, Christ is our exemplar. With his baptism, Christ also covenanted to obey the Father: "He humbleth himself before the Father, and witnesseth unto the Father that he would be obedient unto him in keeping his commandments" (2 Nephi 31:7). Nephi asks, "Can we follow Jesus save we shall be willing to keep the commandments of the Father?" (2 Nephi 31:10). Our covenants bind us into a relationship in which we covenant to "keep his commandments which he has given [us]." It may not be so hard to obey when we're asked to do things that we can see the point of. We are commanded not to kill, commit adultery, steal, take substances that can harm us, and so on. Some things seem obvious, and it hardly takes any humility, any bowing down, to submit ourselves to his will.

The real submission and humility involved in bowing down to God's will comes when we don't understand, when it doesn't make sense. And it's even harder because of the fact that knowledge of God's will often comes through other fallible human beings. Christ delegates his authority. He explained to the apostles: "He that receiveth you receiveth me, and he that receiveth me receiveth him that sent me" (Matthew 10:40).

I was a teenager in northern Virginia in the 1980s. This area had recently known controversies over doctrines and policies of The Church of Jesus Christ of Latter-day Saints that had led to very public excommunications. I remember going to an area conference in a large sports arena as a child in the 1970s. A plane flew by with a banner behind it that said, "Heavenly Mother loves the ERA" (the Equal Rights Amendment was a proposed constitutional amendment that Church leaders spoke out against in 1976). In my youth, along with stacks of missionary pamphlets and copies of the Book of Mormon, we had years' worth of issues of both *Dialogue* and *Sunstone* in our basement that my father felt confident enough to let me read through. I had the chance to think about many of the issues and challenges that still bother people to this day.

One lesson taught in Young Women when I was sixteen or seventeen was a powerful help. Our Young Women president was a wise and inspired woman. She didn't shy away from controversies about women and the priesthood. Instead, she read section 84 of the Doctrine and Covenants with us. I learned about receiving the Lord's servants and receiving all that he hath. And as we read and discussed together, my heart found peace in the Lord's covenant promises even if I didn't have the explanation of why he had organized his Church in this particular way. I knew that I was promised all that the Father hath, and I knew I didn't need to be ordained to an office in the priesthood to receive the promise of his fullness.

Trusting the Lord when we don't understand is bowing down. Trusting that the Lord Jesus Christ spoke through the Prophet Joseph Smith and continues to speak to his living prophet, the President of The Church of Jesus Christ of Latter-day Saints, is bowing down. My submission to Christ's authority is shown when I accept the authority of his servants. We know that they are not perfect. They know that they are not perfect. But part of trusting Christ and having a witness of the restoration of his Church and kingdom in the latter days is knowing that he has chosen his servants. He trusts them. And so, just as we trust him, we can trust them. When we listen to and follow their voice, we are listening to and following his voice. "He that receiveth you receiveth me." Our loyalty to Christ is manifest in our loyalty to his servants.

Exercising faith in Christ to receive his servants takes just that: faith. We choose to receive their word as though from his own mouth (Doctrine and Covenants 1:38; 21:5). And as we do, we qualify ourselves for the greatest blessings that God has. "For he that receiveth my servants receiveth me; and he that receiveth me receiveth my Father; and he that receiveth my Father receiveth my Father's kingdom; therefore all that my Father hath shall be given unto him" (Doctrine and Covenants 84:36–38). I still don't know why men need to be ordained to the priesthood before they can enter into the temple and receive the further covenants and blessings. The apostles have said they don't know either. I just know that I have received those covenants and temple blessings without being ordained, and that is all I need. I am grateful for the privilege of serving in the temple both as a patron and as an ordinance worker. I am confident that all we do in Church service, however we are asked to do it, shows our love and gratitude for our redemption. All service in the Church is worship and none more so than in the temple.

Temple Worship

In addition to the daily choices that reflect our loyalty and grateful submission to our Lord and Redeemer, one dimension of worship that we have in common with the ancient Israelites is temple worship. The verbs *bow down* (ḥwh) and *serve* (ʿābad) were also used to describe how the Israelites responded to God's presence in the temple. When Moses was in the tabernacle, speaking with the Lord, we learn that "all the people saw the cloudy pillar stand at the tabernacle door: and all the people rose up and *worshipped* [ḥwh], every man in his tent door" (Exodus 33:10; emphasis added). Here the verb ḥwh expresses how the people showed their awe and reverence for the presence of the Lord in the tabernacle: they bowed down and prostrated themselves. As is expressed in Psalm 95:6, "O come, let us worship and bow down: let us kneel before the Lord our maker."

Seeing how worship functioned in the world of the Old Testament can help us see the spiritual truths to which the law of Moses pointed and also more fully appreciate living in the dispensation of the fullness of times with the new and everlasting covenant. A certain group of the Israelites, members of the tribe of Levi, were set apart as priests and Levites, those who had priesthood authority for temple service (see Numbers 3:5–10). The verb ʿābad, which can be translated as "worship," also means "to work" and "to serve." Those of the tribe of Levi who were descended from Aaron could serve as priests and officiate in the sacrifices and ordinances of the temple. The priests and Levites were literally temple workers who had the priesthood authority to be in the temple for this service. They worshipped by serving the Lord in the temple. Other Israelites were commanded to come to the temple and to bring their offerings, but under the law of Moses their access to the temple was limited because of their lineage.

Ultimately, the Lord's invitation to serve and worship him is universal: "Make a joyful noise unto the Lord, all ye lands. Serve the Lord with gladness: come before his presence with singing" (Psalm 100:1–2). In our day we see a fulfillment of that psalm. All lands and all people are invited to covenant, be redeemed, and become the Lord's servants. In our day, we can all come and worship as his servants in temples throughout the world. Today all can enjoy this privilege that was once reserved for Levites and priests and come before his presence to worship and praise both as patrons and as ordinance workers.

Bowing down and serving the Lord in the context of temple worship is a commandment, but it is also a way we can express love and gratitude for our redemption. In the ritual action of obedience in temple service, we express and enact our relationship with God. As we ritually enact this relationship of obedience and service, we are better able to go forward to live it out more fully in the rest of our lives. Just as in the sacrament, in the ritual action of temple service we remember the redeeming power and sacrifice of Christ that brings us into the presence of God. We partake of his redemption as we commit to do his will and serve him.

Temple worship is as critical for us as it was for ancient Israel to ritually bow down and serve in the Old Testament temples. In the ritual process of submitting our will to God through temple service, we can let our spirits and minds be changed. Christ was the perfect example of obedience to the Father. He wants us to experience the oneness that he has with the Father in the only way that we can—submitting our will to his. Through ordinances we can learn what it means to worship not only in a ritual context but also in a life of obedience and covenant faithfulness. Through participation in the ordinances, our hope grows that our covenant faithfulness will allow the Lord to bring us back into his presence.

LIFE AS WORSHIP

When we live out a covenant relationship with God, it requires a whole-souled and embodied acceptance of our relationship as his servants to live our lives for him—spirit and body. Embracing the covenant relationship of being the Lord's servant is a full reshaping of ourselves—our minds and bodies oriented to his worship and his service. "And now, Israel, what doth the Lord thy God require of thee, but to fear the Lord thy God, to walk in all his ways, and to love him, and to serve the Lord thy God with all thy heart and with all thy soul" (Deuteronomy 10:12).

Living a life of service and obedience means perpetually being on the Lord's errand. As we live out our covenants we find satisfaction in being the Lord's servants. It is a blessing to be available for the Lord to call on us. We learn to listen with young Samuel, "Speak, Lord; for thy servant heareth" (1 Samuel 3:9). As we seek to serve, we can be a means by which others' prayers are answered. As we serve the Lord we come to know him more fully, "for how knoweth a man the master whom he has not served" (Mosiah 5:13). When we do so with an eye single to God, it is liberating. We are free from seeking others' recognition and can be content, knowing that we "are only in the service of [our] God" (Mosiah 2:17).

But, with our service and obedience, our busyness, we can still sometimes feel stretched and strained. In our hustle and bustle to go and do, we may find our well is running dry. It is easy to slip into simply being active in the Church and feel a hollowness or emptiness inside. Conversely, we may encounter serious challenges that limit our ability to reach out beyond our own survival or the survival of family members. In these times, we may feel that we are failing in our service and our worship. Prolonged health challenges, physical disabilities, and mental illness all can produce a fatigue and desperation that we will never be able to do enough. Worship often is expressed in the outward performances of our lives, the bowing down and serving, and so when our limitations weigh us down, it is time to look again to our Redeemer for a deeper level of our relationship.

CHAPTER 5

THE PRESENCE OF THE LORD

pānîm

y mother was a woman who learned to hear the Lord's voice. She never presided in a Church organization; she was most comfortable behind the scenes. Even though she didn't want any recognition, she found great joy, year after year, in arranging flowers for the chapel on Saturday evenings and then, on Sunday evenings, taking the arrangement to someone in need. Toward the end she gradually lost her ability to be out and doing. She was on dialysis the last ten years of her life, and while she remained physically active for many years after she started dialysis, as time went on repeated infections left her weaker. After a couple of extended hospitalizations, she had to regain her ability to walk and looked decades older than the early sixties that her birthday reported.

Not only did she have limited ability to walk in these years, but she had also lost her cherished independence since she could no longer drive. She became dependent on the thoughtful sisters in the ward who helped

As we seek deeper holiness we keep climbing toward his presence.

her get to her dialysis appointments three times a week. Much of what she had done earlier to serve was no longer an option. There had been a time before she went on dialysis that she worked tirelessly as the director of the stake family history center. She had encouraged, taught, and helped many, many people with family history throughout her life. But toward the end, her concentration and energy were waning. It was hard for her to go online and do family history work. She was gradually losing the ability to do each of the acts of service that had characterized her life.

We can seek and find the Lord when we are busy on his errand, but watching my mother and spending time with her in her declining years helped me learn that there is another, more internal way of seeking and worshipping the Lord. In the Book of Mormon, we read the Lord's invitation: "Come unto me and ye shall partake of the fruit of the tree of life; yea, ye shall eat and drink of the bread and the waters of life freely" (Alma 5:34). All are invited to come and partake of the love of God. Seeking out the presence of the Lord moves us from focusing not only on what we do to obey and sacrifice, but what we are thinking and feeling, who we are. The invitation to partake of the fruit of the tree of life is an invitation to the presence of God—to be with him as we become like him.

One thing that I observed in my mother was purity of heart. In her last year about all she could do was sit and watch television. She loved those cooking shows where you could really learn something and not just be entertained. As I watched her, I was consistently impressed by her sensitivity to anything that might offend the Spirit. Anything unclean or unkind was immediately passed over. She did not hesitate to change the channel. There was no room for it at all. No compromise. No equivocation or justification. No excuses.

Holiness and the Presence of the Lord

One of the most powerful teachings of the Book of Mormon is that no unclean thing can dwell in the presence of God. The doctrine of the presence of God is woven throughout all the teachings in the Book of Mormon, helping us understand not just what we must do but what we must become to be fit for the kingdom. Rather than framing the holiness of becoming clean in narrow, judgmental, or self-righteous terms as it is popularly seen and caricatured, the Book of Mormon presents a vision in which the holiness of being in the presence of God is the source of joy. Being at the tree and partaking of the fruit is being in the presence of God. It is white above all that is white. It is precious above all that is precious. It is sweet above all that is sweet.

When Lehi saw in his dream that his sons Laman and Lemuel did not accept his invitation to come and partake of the tree, he "feared lest they should be cast off from the presence of the Lord" (1 Nephi 8:36). The invitation to come and partake is an invitation to come to the presence of the Lord. In the Old Testament the term *presence* is usually an English translation of the Hebrew word *pānîm*. It literally means "face"—as in one's visage, the front part of one's head—but its usage has a broader sense. When entering the court of a king, one came before his face—that is, came into his presence. The same was true in the temple passages of the Old Testament. The men of Israel were commanded to come before the face of the Lord three times a year during the three required temple festivals: Passover, Pentecost, and Tabernacles (see Exodus 23:14–17). Coming before the face of Lord in the temple described both formal worship in ritual activity and also seeking his presence in that holy place. "My soul thirsteth for God, for the living God: when shall I come and appear before God?" (Psalm 42:2). Longing for the presence of God is part of the quest for holiness.

Holiness and living worthy of being in the presence of God is often portrayed as "life denying." Many would have us believe that enjoyment of life can be cultivated only when we live out our sexuality freely or indulge our senses in the many wonderful substances that bring pleasure. They seek to persuade us that embracing the natural world and our real nature means that we shouldn't be limited by prudish, narrow-minded, or archaic constraints.

Growing up with my mother taught me to see through these kinds of claims. My mother was a free spirit. She sought pleasure in food, art, and nature. She was passionate about watching birds, finding wildflowers, and sitting on the beach and just listening to the sound of the waves. Even when she was in a hospital bed for months recovering from severe infections near the end of her life, she put up a picture of a beach and of the wildflower meadows to remind her why she was doing the physical therapy, why she wanted to walk again.

When we were young, she would, from time to time, take us out of school for adventures, saying that we shouldn't let school interfere with our education. She had a remarkable ability to live free of social constraint. She did try canning and bottling, but when none of us really enjoyed the products and we didn't need it to get by, she went back to buying the fresh fruit that she loved. Once she had survived the years of picky children, her love of food and cooking blossomed. Something that she had always enjoyed became a dedicated pursuit of nuance, flavor, and texture. She was always finding and trying new recipes. She had great joy and pleasure in life.

At the same time, my mother always had a finely tuned sense of holiness. Her joy in nature and her enjoyment of beauty wasn't hedonism. It was worship. She truly did "feel [her] Savior's love in all the world around [her]."[1] She read widely and took us to the library weekly. She almost never watched TV when we were growing up but did enjoy the Olympics, National Geographic specials, and college basketball. She took us to museums and taught us to enjoy all kinds of art. She was not a prudish or narrow-minded woman. She was compassionate and open-minded.

But she could sense when things were not right, when they offended the Spirit. She never spoke ill of others. She stopped us if we tried to. From our youngest years, she corrected us when we did or said things that hurt other people. She had a sensitivity to unkindness that I learned, right near her death, may have been sharpened by arguments between her father and her stepmother. Her mother died when she was nine. What she missed in maternal nurturing she made up for in the way that she loved us and any others that came into her circle. From my mother I learned that enjoying the pleasure of the fruit of the tree of life is part of the plan. It is sweet and delicious. My mother tasted that fruit when she felt the Spirit of the Lord, and she lived so that she stayed worthy to be in the Lord's presence to partake of it.

Symbolism of Temple Holiness

The Israelites lived in a world that was bounded and shaped by their covenant relationship with Jehovah. As part of the covenant relationship, the temple or tabernacle was established as the center around which their lives revolved. It was the center of holiness, the presence of the Lord on the earth. For the Israelites to live worthy to be in the land where the presence of the Lord was found, there were regulations in the law regarding their time, their bodies, their food, and their work. Many of the regulations in the law of Moses were designed to teach the principles of holiness.

The Israelites were tempted to be like their neighbors and to indulge themselves in practices that would betray their relationship with the Lord. In giving the holiness regulations, the Lord was trying to help them remember and be faithful to their covenant relationship. The Sabbath was to be kept holy. They were to separate the holy and the unholy in deciding which food they ate. Priests were held to especially high standards because when they came to the temple, they had to be holy—ritually pure. Touching anything ritually impure would make them ritually impure and unfit to officiate in sacred things. Likewise, the sacrifices offered in the temple were holy, to be eaten only by the priests.

Day after day, the Israelites had to watch themselves. They had to be careful about what they took into their mouths and what they did on the Sabbath day. The Lord gave many specifics in the law of Moses, but he also gave the overarching principle: "Ye shall be holy: for I the Lord your God am holy" (Leviticus 19:2). In particular, the temple or tabernacle was set up in such a way as to illustrate the holiness associated with the presence of the Lord. There was the boundary around the holy courtyard where priests and Levites officiated. There was the building (or tent for the tabernacle) itself, which was divided into rooms of increasing holiness. Priests could enter the Holy Place to pray and maintain the incense altar, showbread, and candelabra, but only the high priest could go into the Holy of Holies, and even he could enter only once a year after careful preparation, including sacrifices to cleanse himself and all of Israel.

The law of Moses was very specific about the criteria for priests who were to officiate in the temple because of the sacredness of approaching the presence of the Lord. The priests had to symbolically represent the Lord and also had to symbolically present the people to the Lord. They had to be ritually holy even as he was holy. The message of the holiness of the temple was reinforced with a focus on wholeness. In Hebrew the term for "perfect" was the same as the word for "whole" or "without blemish": *tāmîm*. Just as the law required that the sacrificial animals be *tāmîm*, whole and unblemished, without any physical impairment, it required the same physical wholeness of priests as is outlined in Leviticus.

These requirements symbolically illustrated spiritual principles by outlining strict boundaries about who could officiate and approach the presence of God. In Leviticus 21 we read some of these prohibitions. Physically impaired priests were forbidden to "come nigh to offer the offerings of the Lord made by fire, . . . to offer the bread of his God, . . . [to] go in unto the veil, [or] come nigh unto the altar, because he hath a blemish; that he profane not my sanctuaries: for I the Lord do sanctify them" (21:21–23). Those who were not whole were not able to serve in the Holy Place or come to the altar. There was a separation between them and the presence of the Lord. As with all things in the law of Moses, the nuanced requirements about the physical pointed to spiritual truths about the nature of God and the nature of holiness. No unclean thing can dwell in the presence of God (see 1 Nephi 10:21; Moses 6:57).

In addition to the limits on the impaired priests to "draw near" to the holiest places of the temple, there are other explicit connections between wholeness and holiness in the Torah for ordinary worshippers. Throughout the regulations of ritual purity, temporary impurity limitations were associated with things that we know are not sins, usually connected with procreation and death. Under the law of Moses, childbirth, menstruation, seminal emissions, and touching dead bodies could make individuals temporarily ritually impure. It seems as though the symbolism of these physical realities of life and death was very powerful, and contact required temporary separation from the presence of God in the temple. With time and certain ritual acts, individuals who had become ritually impure could be made ritually clean again. Likewise, leprosy also rendered individuals unclean, but a person who had been healed could again become clean through a specific temple ritual and offering.

Certain physical deformities, however, represented a permanent condition of being unclean and thus permanently excluded certain worshippers as well as priests from the temple. Here again, there seems to have been powerful symbolism tied to the forces of procreation: those with genital deformity or damage were separated from God's presence. "He that is wounded in the stones, or hath his privy member cut off, shall not enter into the congregation of the Lord" (Deuteronomy 23:1). So, in the world of the Old Testament, men who were eunuchs or who had genital damage would have been excluded from entering the temple.

While this very likely would have encompassed a small number of people, their personal trauma would never have ended. This was not something that would pass. Not only could these individuals not experience family life and posterity as other people, but they were also separated from the house of the Lord. To be categorized as different and unclean would be a sense of self that could not be avoided or wished away. Others could approach the temple to bring offerings on holy days, but not these individuals.

With these regulations of the law of Moses, we see both the symbolism of wholeness and holiness and also the limitations of the law. The healing and access to the presence of God provided by Jesus Christ is prophesied by Isaiah. In Isaiah's prophecies we can understand the law's symbolism of that which is imperfect being separated from the presence of the Lord, but we can also look ahead to the fullness of the redeeming and healing covenant that the Lord wants to establish with all his children. Because of this prophesy we can appreciate how "in the gift of his Son hath God prepared a more excellent way" (Ether 12:11).

This moving passage in Isaiah 56 looks forward to the day when all will be invited into the presence of the Lord, based on their covenant faithfulness.[2] Isaiah speaks of a day when the eunuch who might say "Behold, I am a dry tree" shall hear the Lord's assurance of inheritance and entrance into the temple. "For thus saith the Lord unto the eunuchs that keep my sabbaths, and *choose the things that please me, and take hold of my covenant;* even unto them will I give *in mine house and within my walls* a place and a name better than of sons and daughters: I will give them an everlasting name, that shall not be cut off" (Isaiah 56:3–5; emphasis added).

Unlike in the law of Moses, the Lord promises that those who may see themselves as "a dry tree"—for example, those unable to be a part of a heterosexual marriage—are not permanently separated from his presence. Through Christ and the fullness of his gospel covenant, all those who "choose the things that please me, and take hold of my covenant" are welcomed into his presence. The Lord is aware of all individuals and all kinds of challenges. All are invited to "take hold of [his] covenant." This amazing expression captures our side of a covenant relationship—he metaphorically extends his hand and asks us to *take hold* of his redeeming and sanctifying power.

Taking hold of his covenant is associated here with external obedience, represented by "keeping my sabbaths." But there is also a sense that the Lord wants to be close to those who want to be close to him. Taking hold of his covenant requires not only obedience to the boundaries that he has set but also cultivation of the kind of heart that he has. Seeking to "choose the things that please [him]" is the deeper quest for holiness. When we accept that quest, we seek to become those who love holiness. As we seek to love what the Lord loves and "choose the things that please [him]," we are promised that we shall be given "in mine house and within my walls a place and a name better than of sons and daughters: I will give them an everlasting name, that shall not be cut off." As we seek to increasingly love what God loves, we increasingly receive his name and nature. We increasingly enter into his presence.

Under the law of Moses many limitations of access to the presence of the Lord were independent of agency. People didn't choose which tribe they were born into or whether they would have physical limitations that made them unfit to enter the presence of the Lord. Isaiah foresaw that those who choose the Lord and the things that please him would one day be able to enter into his presence. Isaiah's vision points to deep truths about the restored gospel of Jesus Christ. Those who have been seen as "dry trees" shall be given "a place and a name better than of sons and daughters." Rather than limitation they will experience abundance. The covenants and access to temple blessings in the latter days are now available to all.

Nephi emphasizes, "He inviteth them all to come unto him and partake of his goodness; and he denieth none that come unto him, black and white, bond and free, male and female; and he remembereth the heathen;

and all are alike unto God, both Jew and Gentile" (2 Nephi 26:33). The things that make us feel different from each other are not barriers in the eyes of God. Any human condition that we experience—race, ethnicity, socioeconomic status, sexual orientation, disability, or health condition—any difference of any kind of capacity that leaves us feeling different, alone, unloved, or misunderstood does not keep us out of the presence of God. All are alike unto God. He invites us all to come unto him and partake of his goodness.

ALL ARE INVITED

We can see how these principles play out in worthiness to hold a temple recommend. The question is not if we have experienced same-sex attraction or have a genetic addiction to alcohol but if we are keeping the law of chastity and the Word of Wisdom. Our struggles with any of the commandments associated with temple worthiness are why we have a Redeemer. He is there to bring us out of the captivity of any identity, attitude, addiction, weakness, predisposition, or sin of the natural man part of ourselves that would keep us from the abundant life that he wants to share with us. And in those situations when we, like Paul, ask to have a "thorn in the flesh" removed, he promises that his "grace is sufficient" to be able to continue faithful even when a weakness is not taken away (2 Corinthians 12:7, 9). Christ has paid the price so that we can be freed from the captivity of guilt for anything that we have done. We can walk away from that enslavement if we are willing to keep repenting, keep trying, keep seeking to "take hold of his covenant."

The only time when Christ's ransom price fails to help us is when we don't want to leave the prison. Abinadi's witness of Christ's redemption comes with this warning: "The Lord redeemeth none such that rebel against him and die in their sins." That is the one danger—our refusal. Abinadi explains that those "that have wilfully rebelled against God, that have known the commandments of God, and would not keep them; these are they that have no part in the first resurrection" (Mosiah 15:26). We have to want to live in the freedom that he offers us. We show that desire by our choice to be obedient.

When we reject redemption, we risk dying in our sins, thus losing the desire to ever turn to Christ for life. But none of us have perished in our sins until we permanently lose the desire to repent and to change. Amulek describes this final spiritual death as being "subjected to the spirit of the devil, and he doth seal you his; therefore, the Spirit of the Lord hath withdrawn from you, and hath no place in you, and the devil hath all power over you" (Alma 34:35). This state is the direct opposite of being fully redeemed and being sealed to Christ. For now, all of us are still in play. We are still choosing.

Christ wants us all back. He continues to plead with us not to rebel but to choose redemption and lives of obedience. Until the judgment day, Christ continues to extend his arm of mercy to all of Heavenly Father's children on both sides of the veil, pleading with us to accept the redemption price he has paid with his precious blood. Even in the spirit world, messengers are sent to "proclaim liberty to the captives who were bound, even unto all who would repent of their sins and receive the gospel" (Doctrine and Covenants 138:31).

This amazing vision given to President Joseph F. Smith declares that "it was made known among the dead, both small and great, the unrighteous as well as the faithful, that redemption had been wrought through the sacrifice of the Son of God upon the cross" (Doctrine and Covenants 138:35). Even if we have rejected him before, Christ invites us to choose him. In mortality, we perform vicarious ordinances in temples in hopes that those on the other side will choose faith in the redemption of Christ and accept a new covenant relationship with him. In the spirit world, the message of Christ's redemption is brought "to those who had died in their sins, without a knowledge of the truth, or in transgression, having rejected the prophets" (Doctrine and Covenants 138:32). We just have to want to change. We have to want to be holy.

The standards of holiness are applicable to all. Christ is inviting all to his presence. The choices that we make with our bodies, what substances to partake of and what relationships to have with other people, become a way for us to "choose the things that please [him], and take hold of [his] covenant." When we choose holiness in body and mind, we choose the Lord. We make choices that enable us to enter into his presence.

Continually in His Presence

Another powerful insight into the presence of the Lord in the Book of Mormon is the idea that we can experience his presence always rather than just in temples or when we pass through the veil of mortality. We learn that we are supposed to be partaking of the fruit of the tree now and not just when we die. These insights make it clear that experiencing the presence of the Lord can be part of our covenant relationship on a daily basis and not just a distant promise designed to deny us the joys of mortality in favor of a distant reward.

It is true that many of the passages in which the phrase "the presence of the Lord" appears in the Book of Mormon emphasize judgment and the afterlife. However, some very significant passages with the phrase focus on our condition in this life. These passages are helpful because they show that we don't need to understand being in God's presence only as arriving in the celestial kingdom. These images connect being at the tree and partaking of the fruit as experiencing the presence of the Lord. They show us how the blessings of Christ's Atonement give us access to the divine presence in mortality.

One of the earliest teachings of Lehi, found in 1 Nephi 2:21, explains the relationship of obedience and access to God's presence. Nephi is told, "And inasmuch as thy brethren shall rebel against thee, they shall be cut off from the presence of the Lord." This is set up against the promise of prospering in the land. Later in the Book of Mormon we see a fulfillment of this warning as Alma reminds the people of Ammoniah: "Now I would that ye should remember, that inasmuch as the Lamanites have not kept the commandments of God, they have been cut off from the presence of the Lord. Now we see that the word of the Lord has been verified in this thing, and the Lamanites have been cut off from his presence, from the beginning of their transgressions in the land" (Alma 9:14). Over and over again choices are portrayed as affecting our access to the presence of God *in this life*. Prospering in the land is the opposite of being "cut off from the presence of the Lord." This teaches something very powerful about the promise of prospering in the land—it's not about being rich in money but about being rich in the Spirit.

While the warning of being "cut off from his presence" is a dominant theme in the Book of Mormon, there is a beautiful portrayal of the possibility of enjoying God's presence in this life as well. In a letter from the prophet Helaman to Captain Moroni, we glimpse the way in which we can always enjoy the presence of the Lord. Helaman captures that hope with a simple prayer for Captain Moroni's well-being: "May the Lord our God . . . keep you continually in his presence" (Alma 58:41). These Book of Mormon insights about being in the presence of God in mortality help us move from seeing the presence of God as being tied only to temples or the afterlife.

An important insight in Psalm 51 can help to make explicit how we can continually enjoy the presence of the Lord in this life and thus "prosper in the land." The Psalmist prays: "Cast me not away from thy presence; and take not thy holy spirit from me" (Psalm 51:11). Sometimes we forget the covenant privilege that is ours with the gift of the Holy Ghost. By coming unto Christ with faith, repentance, and partaking of the cleansing power of baptism and the sacrament, we are made fit to be temples of God, to have the presence of the Lord literally *within us* through the gift of the Holy Ghost (see 1 Corinthians 3:16; 6:19). The Holy Ghost is a member of the Godhead. When he is with us, we are experiencing the presence of the Lord. So, seeking to be in the presence of the Lord does prepare us for the next life, but it can also focus us on living worthy to be "continually in his presence" in this life as well (Alma 58:41).

Future or present, in any time frame, we must be clean to enjoy the presence of the Lord. We also must know that we can have no access to his presence on our own. "All are fallen and are lost" (Alma 34:9). Lehi reminds Jacob: "No flesh can dwell in the presence of God, save it be through the merits, and mercy, and grace of the Holy Messiah" (2 Nephi 2:8). Whether we understand being at the tree and partaking of the fruit as enjoying the gift of the Holy Ghost, partaking of the sacrament, entering into holy temples, or being worthy to dwell in celestial realms of glory, access to the presence of the Lord is made possible only in and through Christ's Atonement.

Joy in His Presence

With this framework, the expectations of holiness in the commandments are not warnings about being cut off from some eternal destination. They are instead pointing us to a way of living now. Choosing holiness of mind and body is choosing to dwell in the presence of the Lord now. Choosing anything unclean or offensive to the Spirit of the Lord is choosing to cut ourselves off from the presence of the Lord now. Learning to find joy in holiness rather than experiencing it as the negation of pleasure and enjoyment is part of learning and embodying the deep holiness of becoming Saints.

Not just what we do but who we are becomes our offering to the Lord. We are not sacrificing pleasures of the flesh to please a jealous God, as is so often depicted in hostile caricatures. Holiness is not negative, but positive. Choosing holiness is cultivating the tree that brings forth the fruit that is sweet above all that is sweet. Choosing holiness is savoring the water springing up in us unto everlasting life.

We cannot separate a sincere and humble quest to live lives of holiness from the nature of the Holy One, his way of being. He is Holy. Because he is holy, he is asking us to be holy. We are asked not just to seek forgiveness for the sins that we have committed so that we can be clean, but to seek sanctification so that we increasingly lose the desire to sin. The covenant promise of the "baptism of fire" is given when we are really willing to take upon us the name of Christ (see 2 Nephi 31:13). When we really want to be like him, we have access to the power to become holy.

The gift of the Holy Ghost is the means by which the sanctifying, purifying influence of Christ's Atonement becomes available to us. When we choose holiness, we choose to invite that cleansing power into our lives. Becoming sanctified literally means becoming holy. *Sanctus* is simply the Latin term for "holy." As we seek to become Saints in thought and feeling, we are seeking to take his name and nature upon us in the deepest sense of the term. He is the Holy One. We are seeking to receive his nature and to become holy, even as he is holy.

Faith produces repentance. Part of the faith required in this quest for holiness is to believe that he wants us to be happy. Part of what we need to know as we increasingly seek holiness is a conviction that God's nature is not only holiness, but also happiness. On this point, again, the Book of Mormon gives us the strongest witness. It warns us that if we don't want what Christ is offering, we will never find what we thought we were looking for in life. Alma warned Corianton that we can't fool ourselves that we will be "restored from sin to happiness," because "wickedness never was happiness" (Alma 41:10).

Alma had a lot of personal experience with getting out of the bonds of iniquity through faith in the redemption of Christ. He wanted to make sure that his son understood that it is our very *way of being* when we are unredeemed that makes us miserable. "All men that are in a state of nature, or I would say, in a carnal state, are in the gall of bitterness and in the bonds of iniquity; they are without God in the world, and they have gone contrary to the nature of God; therefore, they are in a state contrary to the nature of happiness" (Alma 41:11). Samuel the Lamanite also warned that unless we change and start wanting what God wants, someday we will know that "[we] have sought all the days of [our] lives for that which [we] could not obtain; and [we] have sought for happiness in doing iniquity, which thing is contrary to the nature of that righteousness which is in our great and Eternal Head" (Helaman 13:38). Misery is an existential problem—the way we are is the problem itself; repentance and redemption through Christ is the existential solution—only he can change our natures.

Satan's most potent lie is that holiness is contrary to happiness. Instead, as we seek to be worthy to be in the presence of the Lord, we find that being where he is helps us to become as he is. We come to find that as we become more like him, we have greater happiness. This quest to be worthy to enter the presence of the Lord opens up a better way of being, both in mortality and the eternities.

Amulek used an ancient image to describe what we are moving toward in our daily struggle for sanctification. He reminded us, "the Lord hath said he dwelleth not in unholy temples, but in the hearts of the righteous doth he dwell; yea, and he has also said that the righteous shall sit down in his kingdom, to go no more out; but their garments should be made white through the blood of the Lamb" (Alma 34:36). The image of "sitting down" in his presence to go no more out may feel elusive in mortality, but as we think through the terms and images associated with "sitting down" in the presence of the Lord, we increasingly move our vision toward his exalted nature and what he intends for us.

Notes

1. See K. Newell Dayley, "I Feel My Savior's Love," in *Children's Songbook* (Salt Lake City: The Church of Jesus Christ of Latter-day Saints, 1989), 74.
2. I have been indebted for many years to Daniel Belnap for his insights on this Isaiah passage, now published as "'The Lord God Which Gathereth the Outcasts' (Isaiah 56:3–8)," *Religious Educator* 19, no. 3 (2018): 117–36.

CHAPTER 6

SITTING ENTHRONED
yāšab

Sitting down is a powerful expression of stability and permanence. It is made even more powerful with the Hebrew verb *yāšab* (pronounced *yashab*) that, in connection with kings and deity, means "sitting enthroned." Kings and queens take the throne when they receive the right to rule. The Holy of Holies in the temple was essentially Jehovah's throne room on earth. "The Lord is in his holy temple, the Lord's throne is in heaven" (Psalm 11:4). Amulek's vision that "the righteous shall sit down in his kingdom, to go no more out" (Alma 34:36) may give us hope that someday things will be settled and fixed and permanent in our relationship with the Lord. We will have arrived! We will have endured to the end in our covenant keeping! We will be able to "to sit with [Christ] in [his] throne, even as [he] also overcame, and [is] set down with [his] Father in his throne" (Revelation 3:21).

But the same vision of sitting down in the kingdom, to go no more out, might also lead us to despair that we'll never arrive. While we want to

FINDING CHRIST IN THE COVENANT PATH

Christ's redemption assures us that through covenant faithfulness we can sit down with him on his throne and receive all that the Father hath. He has promised that "whoso cometh in at the gate and climbeth up by me shall never fall; . . . they shall come forth with songs of everlasting joy" (Moses 7:53).

live out our covenant with lives of obedience and to seek for lives of holiness, we can easily feel that our efforts are too erratic. We know the times we fail to listen to promptings. We know the times we say impatient and unkind things that we wish we could take back. We each know our personal weaknesses and struggles that seem to drag us down and lead us to repent yet again in an effort to find peace and be free.

When I was a young girl, I learned the steps of repentance. My parents and Primary leaders taught me that the steps included recognizing we did something wrong, apologizing, and never doing it again. I very clearly remember sitting in our kitchen after a scolding and being taught about this. I remember how much that idea of repentance puzzled me. I thought and thought but was stumped. When I hit my younger brother, I could see that it was wrong. I knew I could apologize to him, and I did. But I just couldn't fathom never doing it again. My sense of self was based entirely on my feelings and actions of that age of my life. I couldn't see myself being or becoming a person who wouldn't have an inclination to punch or tease or hassle him.

I look back now and smile at myself. It seems so silly to think that I would always be that childish, impulsive, and bossy older sister. I'm not perfect, but I honestly have no desires to hit my younger brother. Yes, he is now about eight inches taller than I am and the father of five sons, but that is not the explanation. We are friends. I love him. I might sometimes still be the bossy older sister, but I hope even that has mellowed with the years. We are still sister and brother, but our relationship is dramatically different than it was during the years in which my sister and I would throw the big beanbag chair over him and then jump on him. He survived. My sister and I repented. We all grew up together. Each, in our way and with our own experiences, learned about the redeeming love of the Lord and felt a change of heart. We all still read the Book of Mormon and seek to build the kingdom. Our relationship as siblings has an added dimension because we share a love for the Lord as well as each other.

The vision that not only can we sit down in the kingdom but can also sit down together in love is not an inevitable result of the human condition. It is a vision of redeemed humanity. Relationships where resentment, emotional scarring, and pain dominate interactions are part of what it means to live in a fallen world. Christ could see that this was not who we really are. He could see that this was not where we belong, eternally trapped in relationships that Jean-Paul Sartre famously described in his play *No Exit*. "Hell is other people." Instead, Christ came down to us in our broken, fallen state to lift us up and show us that we belong in a more elevated state. Christ leads us to heavenly life, a life increasingly filled with others on a celestial journey.

One day in my early twenties, I was in the dressing room of the Provo Temple. I saw a woman I knew to have served many missions in her older years. She impressed me that day by reaching out to a sister she didn't know in a kind, loving, and genuine way, saying, "here, let me help you." She tucked the tag back in on that sister's dress, smiled, and touched her on the shoulder. Something inside me wanted to believe that someday I could look outside myself, see others' needs, and fearlessly and graciously lift them up and help them along. I knew that I was still absorbed with myself and my own problems. I knew that my shyness could be paralyzing and that it kept me locked away from reaching out to others. But when I saw that gracious, loving action, I wanted to be able to do that. I wanted to be the person who would and could do that for others.

Christ came to show us who we could be. When we are taking the name of Christ upon us, we can show others who he is and who they can become. Faith in the Lord Jesus Christ can loose the deepest bonds of all, the ones that keep us from repenting because we just can't believe that we can ever be the person who, metaphorically, will never punch our brother again. Believing in the redemption of Jesus Christ makes real repentance possible. Believing in the redemption of Jesus Christ is believing that we can someday be the person who has "no more disposition to do evil, but to do good continually" (Mosiah 5:2).

The way that Christ's redemption wakes us up to this new sense of self can "blow our minds," shocking us into a new way of thinking. Our fallen selves know, deep down, that we are wretched. Our fallen selves know that we have hurt others and deserve to be hurt in return. Our fallen selves can't imagine being different or wanting different things. We know that we are in the dust and that we deserve to be in the dust.

God takes us from the dust and shows us that we belong on thrones instead. Hannah, the mother of the prophet Samuel, expressed God's power to reverse our state and radically change our vision of ourselves. Her prayer emphasizes that we can be lifted up to a glorified state and shows the glory of our Deliverer rather than of our own merits: "He raiseth up the poor out of the dust, and lifteth up the beggar from the dunghill, to set them among princes, *and to make them inherit the throne of glory*" (1 Samuel 2:8; emphasis added). By telling us we can be worthy to inherit the throne of glory, Christ is fracturing our own narratives of ourselves. In our heart of hearts, we may think that we are the poor in the dust or the beggar on the dunghill, but he does not see us that way. He does not leave us there. He calls us to arise from the dust and to sit enthroned.

This is the invitation that Isaiah records in Isaiah 52: "Shake thyself from the dust; arise, and sit down [*yāšab*, "sit enthroned"], O Jerusalem: loose thyself from the bands of thy neck, O captive daughter of Zion"

(52:2). We feel we are captive to our weaknesses, even when we know that a redemption price has been paid. So Christ doesn't just say, "Leave captivity!" He says, "Sit enthroned! This is who you really are. This is where you belong. Arise and inherit the throne prepared for you in the mansions of your Father."

Christ's ransom for our souls and his invitation to come and sit with him on his throne is a shocking refutation of everything that we feel we deserve. He is telling us that he has not only bought us out of bondage, but also that he is lifting us up to thrones of glory in the presence of his Father. His love for us, his vision of who we are and who we can become, is so radically different from our fears and doubts, our regrets and self-recrimination, that it can rewrite our vision of ourselves and our lives.

I experienced a witness of this "mind-blowing" love in probably the darkest moment of my life. As I mentioned before, I like to do everything right. Maybe it comes with being the oldest, but I always want to be the good example, the model child. About a year into my mission, I was assigned as a trainer. This was the ultimate opportunity to be a model and good example. And I failed. But not because I didn't try. I worked and worked, trying to do everything the right way. But I was not possessed of the love that could nurture our companionship. All my efforts to do everything right had the opposite effect I had intended because I was focused on myself. It came to the point where I knew I had to do what I never would have dreamed I would need to do. I called the mission president and told him that we needed an emergency transfer.

She was moved to a city with one of the most loving and gracious sisters in the mission. I was moved to a city with a kind and patient sister who didn't freak out when I cried myself to sleep at night from the shame and the regret of everything that I had done wrong when I tried to do everything right. One of those nights, I had a life-changing experience. I don't know if it was a dream or a vision or a thought. But I could clearly see myself back in Virginia, entering our dining room from the back porch. I came with all my regret and shame. I came feeling like a failure. And there, standing in the dining room right near the door to the kitchen was my mother. Her arms were open, and she said, "I love you anyway." The witness of Christ's redeeming love that I felt through that vision of my mother and her love became the bedrock of my life.

"I love you anyway." Christ knows us. He knows what we have done. He knows what we have felt, what we have thought, and he loves us anyway. That is the message of redeeming love. He laid aside his crown for our soul. He came down to earth from heaven to show us who we are and where we belong. His suffering and death encompassed our sins, weaknesses, and mistakes. Even when we try our best and it all falls apart, he suffered for us. When we lie down on the job and don't do our part, he suffered for that too.

Our Foundation

There is no other way to be saved, only in and through the atoning blood of Jesus Christ. His redeeming love must be our foundation. We cannot build on our own righteousness. We can and must build lives of holiness to honor his name. We can and must walk in the light to thank him for buying us out of the darkness of slavery to sin. But whatever efforts we make to do good and be good, it must always be on the foundation of his unchangeable love.

In the New Testament, Paul uses the image of being rooted in Christ's love to describe the foundation we are given. We are able to grow because we receive the nourishment we need from Christ. Paul prays that "[God] would grant you, according to the riches of his glory, to be strengthened with might by his Spirit in the inner man" (Ephesians 3:16). When we feel the Spirit, we feel a witness of the love of God that gives us strength to do and be what we have covenanted to be. Paul continues this prayer—"that Christ may dwell in your hearts by faith" (3:17). Having Christ dwell in our hearts is not an image we use much as Latter-day Saints because we know that, as the Risen Lord, he has a glorified, resurrected body. Nonetheless, this feeling of being rooted, grounded, and established in the love of God can symbolically be compared to having Christ dwell in our hearts. His love for us and his vision of us as exalted beings, sitting with him on his throne, radiate the light that can drive out the darkness of doubt and discouragement. Paul describes this condition as "being rooted and grounded in love" (3:17).

Being rooted and grounded in the love of Christ, we can continue along the covenant path. We can grow up into the exalted state that Christ sees in us. Paul prays, "That ye, being rooted and grounded in love, may be able to comprehend with all saints what is the breadth, and length, and depth, and height; and to know the love of Christ, which passeth knowledge, that ye might be filled with all the fulness of God" (Ephesians 3:17–19). The fullness of God. That is the promise: being filled with all the fullness of God, all the Father hath. That is our inheritance. That is what God has sworn with his oath and covenant to give us if we are willing to receive (see Doctrine and Covenants 84:33–39).

The Invitation to Become

We don't deserve it. We don't earn it. The gift of Christ's redeeming love comes to us not just to start us on the path home, but also to give us strength, power, and desire to continue on the journey. He invites us to "arise, and sit down on a throne" (Isaiah 52:2). He finds us in the dust, and we may not believe the invitation at first. It is too outrageous, too far-fetched. We don't belong "at the right hand of God in the kingdom of heaven, to sit down with Abraham, and Isaac, and with Jacob and with all our holy fathers, to go no more out" (Helaman 3:30). But he has come to invite us to sit down with them and with him. He is telling us that we are welcome, that we belong.

Mormon talks about this promise. He uses the phrase *sitting down* to frame his assurance that "the Lord is merciful unto all who will, in the sincerity of their hearts, call upon his holy name" (Helaman 3:27). Mormon doesn't say that Christ is merciful to those who have always been perfect in keeping their covenants. Mormon doesn't say that Christ is merciful to those who are always diligent in keeping his commandments.

Mormon doesn't say that Christ is merciful to those who have never done anything to offend the Spirit of the Lord. Christ is merciful to us when we are sincere. Christ is merciful to us when we "call upon his holy name." Our confidence must be in his nature and his name, not in our own. We will call upon his holy name when we know that he is our Kinsman-Redeemer and that he will come and get us, no matter how horrible the trouble we've gotten ourselves into.

For any number of reasons we may find ourselves captive and in the dust, but we have a choice. Our choice, our only choice for getting out of captivity, is to "call upon his holy name," to exercise faith in his redeeming power, over and over again (Helaman 3:27). When we exercise faith in Christ, he opens us up to the power of his redemption and the power of his exaltation. He wants to exalt us to a higher status, and he will, if we let him and if we keep asking and keep believing. "The gate of heaven is open unto all, even to those who will believe on the name of Jesus Christ, who is the Son of God" (3:28). As we "lay hold upon the word of God," we find that it is "quick and powerful," leading us across the "everlasting gulf of misery" (3:29). It can be a long journey, but he is patient and faithful as we keep struggling and stumbling forward along the path.

In the end, it comes back to what we want. We have to want to get out of the gulf of misery. We have to want to "lay hold upon the word of God" and go where it is taking us. We have to be willing to come to a new place. We have to be willing to be different and feel different. When we hold on and follow the word of God, we find that it will "land [our] souls, yea [our] immortal souls, at the right hand of God in the kingdom of heaven, to *sit down* with Abraham, and Isaac, and with Jacob, and with all our holy fathers, to go no more out" (Helaman 3:30). He can get us there. He will get us there. We just have to want to be there enough to leave our "gulf of misery."

Settling Down

Sitting implies permanence and stability. But sometimes we just fall for the novel and the exciting. It's like being in a classroom when everyone is all excited and the teacher says, "OK everybody, it's time to settle down." We love the buzz of something new and different. Controversy and scandal catch our attention. It's fun and entertaining to have new things to talk about and speculate about. It's a break from the routine.

Following the covenant path can feel routine, but part of growing up in life and part of growing up in Christ is learning to find joy and satisfaction in the routine. Stability may seem like the enemy when we're a thrill-seeking teen, but refusing to settle down leads us to miss out on being at home in God's presence. If we're always seeking out new sensations and diversions, we won't settle down to be present and enjoy the simple joys of the Spirit.

There's a phrase in the scriptures that has several meanings: "entering into the rest of the Lord." In its most lofty and sacred sense it describes becoming people who are worthy to enter into the physical presence of the Lord in mortality (see Doctrine and Covenants 84:19–24). But within the layers of meaning, entering into the "fullness of his glory" doesn't have to be an event as much as a feeling of being settled and grounded in Christ's love and his covenant promises. It's the hope that follows faith. We're not there yet. We're still on the journey. We're still traveling down the covenant path. But we know that we will arrive. We have confidence in the direction that we are going and that our efforts are pleasing to the Lord. We don't panic. We're not bored. We don't keep asking, "Are we there yet?" We don't have to see the throne of glory to know that it is ours.

In Moroni 7, Mormon spoke to a group of people that he said were "the peaceable followers of Christ, and that have obtained a sufficient hope by which ye can enter into the rest of the Lord, from this time henceforth until ye shall rest with him in heaven" (Moroni 7:3). I think that is the goal in mortality: becoming the peaceable followers of Christ. As our faith in Christ grows, we follow him. We make and keep covenants. We live lives of worship, bowing down and serving, being humble enough to do things his way even when we may not understand. We live lives of holiness, honoring him by applying his atoning blood to become clean and to purify our desires. Having faith we "lay hold upon every good thing" (7:25) and "cleave unto every good thing" (7:28).

But since we're not perfect, we won't always be consistent in this learning process of a journey. We may increasingly want to cleave unto every good thing, but our actions don't always match our aspirations. How can we be settled then if we ourselves are not constant? Faith in Christ produces something that stabilizes us when the fruits of our faith are sometimes a little erratic. Mormon explains "if a man have faith he must needs have hope; for without faith there cannot be any hope" (Moroni 7:42). Our hope is the internal product of faithful living. Even if we are not perfect in everything, our confidence that *he* is grows and grows. Hope is the fruit of faith. Moroni describes this "hope [which] cometh of faith" as "an anchor to the souls of men" (Ether 12:4). As we keep looking to Christ and keep calling on his holy name, we find that he is there for us. We know that his promises are sure. He is our Redeemer. He doesn't leave us stranded.

So, Mormon asks, "What is it that ye shall hope for?" And then he gives us the best possible answer, the answer that we can rely on to bring hope to our souls: "Behold I say unto you that ye shall have hope through the atonement of Christ and the power of his resurrection, to be raised unto life eternal, and this because of your faith in him according to the promise" (Moroni 7:41). Christ's promise is sure. We trust in the covenant because we trust in him. We can have confidence that even if we have slipped and fallen, he is there to raise us up and put us back on the path. If we have sold ourselves, he has already paid the price for our release. We will be "raised unto life eternal" because he is our Redeemer. He is our covenant Father. He can and will bring us home. Our "faith in him according to the promise" gives us the courage to get up and keep going down the covenant path. He is the source of our stability. He is the source of our hope. Because his promises are sure, we can settle down and not be tossed about by the novelty and controversy that keep everyone else jittery and agitated.

SITTING DOWN WITH CHRIST

In his visit to the Americas, the Savior gave us a glimpse of the exalted state to which we are being led. He used the imagery of sitting down to describe the full change of status and condition of the three disciples who were translated. "And for this cause ye shall have fulness of joy; and *ye shall sit down in the kingdom of my Father*; yea, your joy shall be full, even as the Father hath given me fulness of joy; and ye shall be even as I am, and I am even as the Father; and the Father and I are one" (3 Nephi 28:10). The promise of becoming "even as I am" and "even as the Father" is, is the fullest possible sense of being exalted, or lifted up, to a new status. This is the end to which we are progressing on our journey of discipleship.

Obtaining this exalted and divine state and condition requires us to be filled with charity and to take on the divine nature. It's a long journey, but we can have hope. We see this clearly taught in the Lord's promise to Moroni in the book of Ether. Moroni first acknowledges the sobering truth that "except men shall have charity they cannot inherit that place which thou hast prepared in the mansions of thy Father" (Ether 12:34). The Lord proceeds to console Moroni in the face of others' weakness and even in the face of his own weakness: "And it came to pass that the Lord said unto me: If they have not charity it mattereth not unto thee, thou hast been faithful; wherefore, thy garments shall be made clean. And because thou hast seen thy weakness thou shalt be made strong, *even unto the sitting down in the place which I have prepared in the mansions of my Father*" (Ether 12:37). Moroni was being invited to a throne of glory that was a *way* of being as much as a *place* to be. He was promised that he would be made strong enough to sit down on the throne prepared for him.

Moroni wasn't blessed for having no weakness. He was blessed for seeing his weakness. That is always where we have to start. That is how the process works. We must start by acknowledging that we need help, that we need a Redeemer. Having the humility and faith to ask for his grace opens up the door to all that we need to do and to be. Moroni was taught, "if men come unto me I will show unto them their weakness. I give unto men weakness that they may be humble; and my grace is sufficient for all men that humble themselves before me; for if they humble themselves before me, and have faith in me, then will I make weak things become strong unto them" (Ether 12:27). Christ will redeem us. Christ will exalt us. But he can't exercise faith for us. He can't repent for us. We have to choose him. We have to trust him. We have to want to be where he is and how he is more than we want to stay where we are now.

Being exalted to sit upon the throne requires not only leaving behind the captivity and dust of sin but also putting on the beautiful garments of righteousness and sitting down upon the throne of God's glorious and godly nature. Here is the symbolic invitation to live a better way: "Awake, awake; put on thy strength, O Zion; put on thy beautiful garments, O Jerusalem, the holy city: for henceforth there shall no more come into thee the uncircumcised and the unclean. Shake thyself from the dust; arise, and sit down [enthroned], O Jerusalem: loose thyself from the bands of thy neck, O captive daughter of Zion. For thus saith the Lord, Ye have sold yourselves for nought; and ye shall be redeemed without money" (Isaiah 52:1–3). The Lord knows that we've made mistakes. But he reaches out to save us, to buy us out of the bondage we cannot leave on our own. As Lehi testified, "There is no flesh that can dwell in the presence of God, save it be through the merits, and mercy, and grace of the Holy Messiah" (2 Nephi 2:8). His grace is sufficient, if we are willing to rise up and become what he sees in us. His redemption is there to reclaim us and to take us to where we belong, sitting on the throne of the covenant promise of exaltation. We do serve him as his servants when we are redeemed, but he has bought us so that we can become kings and queens, sitting on an exalted throne.

As we're getting used to being redeemed and living lives of holiness, these garments of righteousness might feel like an awkward fit at first. They might not be fashionable. They might make us stand out or seem old fashioned. We might be tempted to adjust them, to take shortcuts in keeping the commandments. We might be tempted to leave them behind when we want to go somewhere they don't fit in. It's easy to forget that we were once captive and sitting in the dust. We may start to see ourselves as limited by the covenant relationship that makes us his servants, bowing down and doing God's will and not our own. It's easy to resent his expectations of holiness and righteousness. Do we really have to wear these robes of righteousness all the time?

We have to remember that we were in bondage. We were all captive. We sold ourselves for naught. Our Redeemer found us in captivity and invited us to "arise from the dust" (2 Nephi 1:14) and to "shake off the awful chains by which ye are bound" (1:13). But, in addition to liberating us from the bondage of sin, he also invites us to sanctify ourselves, to "put on [our] beautiful garments" and to sit down upon the throne of godliness and righteousness (Isaiah 52:1).

Being clothed with righteousness is a temple image that shows us that God wants to give us the kind of nature that he has, if we are willing to keep moving along the path to receive that gift. As we gradually feel greater desires to do good and be good, then we can say with all our hearts, "My soul shall be joyful in my God; for he hath clothed me with the garments of salvation, he hath covered me with the robe of righteousness" (Isaiah 61:10).

When we attend the temple, we accept the invitation to ritually sit down as kings and queens. When we discard anything filthy from our lives, we accept the invitation to sit down as kings and queens and allow ourselves to be clothed with the robe of righteousness. Through the daily, upward journey to receive what Christ is giving us, we look ahead to the day when we can fully participate in the promise that "the righteous shall have a perfect knowledge of their enjoyment, and their righteousness, being clothed with purity, yea, even with the robe of righteousness" (2 Nephi 9:14).

Just as we are invited to put on "robes of righteousness" that are external representations of an internal state, so the "throne" upon which God sits and reigns is the "throne" of his righteousness and holiness. The Psalmist taught that "righteousness and judgment are the habitation of his throne" (Psalm 97:2) and that "God sitteth upon the throne of his holiness" (Psalm 47: 8). His throne is not where he is as much as how he is.

As we receive the redemption that Christ offers, we gradually overcome the natural man part of ourselves. In that process, we leave behind the dust and captivity of sin and mortal limitations and are lifted up to become righteous and holy through faith and repentance. As we believe Christ's vision of who we are and what we can become, we prepare ourselves to receive the exalted promise: "Sit with me in my throne, even as I also overcame, and am set down with my Father in his throne" (Revelation 3:21). As we become like him and take on the divine nature, we prepare ourselves to "sit down in the kingdom of my Father; . . . and ye shall be even as I am, and I am even as the Father; and the Father and I are one" (3 Nephi 28:10).

PART TWO

CHRIST, OUR RANSOM PRICE

"Behold the Lamb of God, which taketh away the sin of the world" (John 1:29). Hieronymus Bosch, *Christ Carrying the Cross*, detail, ca. 1500, Kunsthistorisches Museum, Vienna. Directmedia Publishing GmbH (CC0 1.0).

CHAPTER 7

EXPLORING MEDIEVAL IMAGES

he plan of redemption requires a Redeemer, a Redeemer who pays a price to buy his family members out of bondage. We need to trust our Redeemer, and we need to trust his ransom price. When we wonder if we can really escape from whatever traps us, we need to know that we are really forgiven, that we are really free. Even after we make covenants, some part of us may feel that we deserve our punishment, our banishment, our captivity. Some part of us may feel that the forces of chaos and evil will keep us trapped in an existence without peace or hope.

To combat our constant inclination to fear and doubt, our Redeemer paid a price that should be enough to keep us from ever wondering if we are free and if we can move forward out of our prisons. It should be enough to keep us from ever wondering if we are worth something. Our Redeemer gave himself as our Ransom. As Peter said, "Ye were not redeemed with corruptible things, as silver and gold, . . . but with the precious blood of Christ, as of a lamb without blemish and without spot:

who verily was foreordained before the foundation of the world" (1 Peter 1:18–20). That is the plan. It has always been the plan. Christ was foreordained as our ransom price—as our vicarious, substitutionary sacrifice. This plan of redemption is God's ancient message of hope that he has been trying to communicate through the ages.

Throughout time, God's ordinances have pointed to the price paid for our deliverance. It is important to participate in the ordinances, but it is even more helpful when we can also behold the ransom price that they point to. Adam was obedient and offered sacrifices without understanding, but when he was given an explanation about why he was offering sacrifices, the angel said, "This thing is a similitude of the sacrifice of the Only Begotten of the Father, which is full of grace and truth" (Moses 5:7). The firstlings of their flocks pointed to the sacrifice of the Only Begotten of the Father. Adam and Eve and their descendants needed to continue with the external offerings, but they also needed to *behold* in that physical symbol of a sacrificed animal the death of the Son of God.

Opportunities for repeated practice in beholding the death of Christ were amplified with the law of Moses as the sacrifices became even more nuanced and elaborate. But again, the human tendency to go through the motions without reflecting on the meaning of symbolic action is something that plagued the children of Israel, as it can plague us. It can be easy to believe that our obedience in performing the ordinances is what saves us. This is particularly ironic when we consider that the ordinances themselves are supposed to point to our need for deliverance and redemption. The priests of King Noah were convinced that their obedience saved them, but Abinadi repeated Isaiah's prophecy of the One who would be "wounded for our transgressions" and "bruised for our iniquities" (Mosiah 14:5). Abinadi declared that "God himself shall come down among the children of men, and shall redeem his people" (Mosiah 15:1). Our Redeemer himself came down to be our Ransom.

If we're confident since we've been baptized and been to the temple that our obedience to those commandments is what has saved us, then we find ourselves missing the point as much as the priests of King Noah.

If we're fearful that we will never be able to keep all the commandments and please God, then we're missing the point too. Our confidence can't be in ourselves. The ordinances are there to point us to Christ and to increase our confidence in the price that he paid as our Redeemer. So our challenge is not just to participate, but to *behold*, to take meaning out of the ordinances, to see them pointing us to Christ's expiatory suffering and death.

In 1 Nephi, chapter 11, Nephi was trying to understand the meaning of the tree his father had seen. He was shown the birth, ministry, and death of Jesus Christ. But the way Nephi took meaning out of what he saw, the way he *beheld*, was through the insight of revelation, the revelation of Christ's role as our Ransom. When Nephi "looked and beheld the virgin again, bearing a child in her arms," he was told by the angel: "Behold the Lamb of God, yea, even the Son of the Eternal Father" (1 Nephi 11:20–21). This revelation of Christ as the Lamb of God, the sacrifice prepared before the creation of the world, allowed Nephi to behold his ministry and death as the great vicarious gifts that they were. Nephi beheld the Lamb of God going forth to be baptized. Nephi beheld the Lamb of God going forth to minister and heal. Nephi didn't just see a human life and death—he "beheld the Lamb of God" taken, judged, and finally "lifted up upon the cross and slain for the sins of the world" (11:32–33).

Nephi was able to behold the Father's ancient message of hope in the life and death of Jesus Christ because he beheld him as the Lamb of God, our ransom price. This is the message the Savior stressed in his postmortal ministry; he invited the people at Bountiful to feel his wound marks "that ye may know that I am the God of Israel, and the God of the whole earth, and have been slain for the sins of the world" (3 Nephi 11:14). As he defined his gospel, Christ stressed, "I came into the world to do the will of my Father, because my Father sent me. And my Father sent me that I might be lifted up upon the cross" (3 Nephi 27:13–14). This is the good news. The Lamb of God was "lifted up upon the cross and slain for the sins of the world." Before the coming of Christ it took thought and effort to behold Christ's vicarious sacrifice in the death of animals. In our day we have different ordinances, but the purpose is the same.

In my freshman composition class, we studied travel literature. I had written an essay about Graham Greene's novel *Travels with My Aunt*. My instructor made a comment that I have never forgotten. "You have set up a good frame, but I want to see the picture inside." I had written about the novel without really digging in and analyzing the primary material itself. When we study the gospel, we often do the same thing. We are very excited about the context and the historical details, but the frame sometimes overshadows the picture. We could profitably discuss many specifics about the law of Moses or give details about Christ's historical ministry and the events of his suffering and death, but these are ways of approaching these topics that we have all developed over years of scripture study and Gospel Doctrine classes. If we feel that we're still focusing on the frame and not the picture, then let's come at this from a different angle.

For the purposes of practicing *beholding* the suffering and death of Christ, we don't need more historical details. Even people who saw the historical suffering and death of Christ still needed to look beyond the events to see the meaning of his death as our vicarious substitute. Learning to behold is a critical tool because God's ancient message of hope is primarily communicated through images and symbols. We can get better at beholding. We can get better at seeing Christ as our ransom price in the ordinances and the scriptures, but we have to practice. Developing skills in sports or the arts sometimes comes by isolating a particular skill rather than just continuing to play the game or a piece of music. Our skill in finding meaning in the scriptures and the ordinances can improve with practice as well. When we focus on beholding Christ as the Lamb of God, when we focus closely on his vicarious suffering on our behalf, we can get better at seeing the picture rather than the frame, we can become more attuned to God's ancient message of hope.

To keep our focus on Christ as our Ransom, in this second part of the book I will shift from a more typical path of expanding on Old

Testament symbolism pointing to Christ or telling more about the New Testament setting to instead explore what we can learn from medieval images of Christ. To me, one of the most helpful ways I have found to behold Christ and see the picture within the frame has come from studying medieval religious art. Late medieval religious thought, experience, and artistic expression was squarely focused on Christ's suffering and death. The late medieval emphasis on seeing, being changed by, and embodying Christ's Atonement has messages that resonate strongly in the restored gospel. Exploring the late medieval use of symbolism can help our minds more easily see the symbols in the gospel ordinances and scriptures. It may feel like a detour after our previous discussion of ancient words, but this has been my journey. I finished a master's thesis focused on covenant and redemption in the writings of Paul and was sure that my next step was studying baptism in the early Christian period. But, it's almost like saying, "A funny thing happened on the way to becoming a professor of religious education at BYU–Hawaii." I came to see Christ in the ordinances and scriptures more fully in an unexpected way. Here is some of my story.

After our first year of marriage and my master's degree in ancient Near Eastern studies at BYU, my husband and I were in Southern California for PhD programs. My husband started his program first. I did long-term temporary office work that first year as we had been hoping to have children. I had been working at a law firm as a legal secretary and, while that can be a rewarding profession, I realized it wouldn't be a good fit for me for the rest of my life if I were to keep working. I decided to begin a PhD program and just see what happened as time went on.

I started the Christian history program at Claremont Graduate University the next year. I started studying Coptic and more Greek. During that first semester in graduate school, my husband and I went to Provo, Utah, for a short trip. I was presenting at the Sperry Symposium based on the material in my master's thesis, and we were excited to return for a short visit. While in Provo, we went up to the BYU Bookstore, where I had an experience that changed the direction of my life.

I went to buy a Greek grammar book in the textbook section and, as I picked it up, I had a heavy feeling. It just wasn't making me happy, but I felt dutiful and put it in my shopping basket. I then walked down the row of bookcases along the far wall. Near the end, in a corner, I found a full set of shelves from floor to ceiling filled with books on medieval history and culture. I had such an enormous sensation of enthusiasm and real joy. I stayed and just looked at all those books. Something was happening to me to change what I wanted to do with my doctoral studies. To this day, I have no idea what those books were there for, but I will never forget how I felt looking at them. I told my mother about the experience later, and being a woman very close to the Spirit and spiritual promptings, she asked why I even bought the Greek grammar book.

That is how I came to focus on medieval Christianity in my graduate studies. My background in the ancient Near East and Jerusalem made pilgrimage and sacred place a recurring theme through those studies. I eventually wrote my dissertation on how in the later Middle Ages the Franciscans changed Jerusalem pilgrimage into a meditation on Christ's suffering and death. Many of us are familiar with this influence, having heard of the Via Crucis or Way of the Cross in Jerusalem and also the practice of the Stations of the Cross found in many churches. Starting with this dissertation research, I have spent a lot of time in the last half of my life studying late medieval devotional art and thinking about the role it played in this cultural and religious world.

My professional life now focuses on teaching religious education courses such as the New Testament and Jesus Christ and the Everlasting Gospel, but I am different because of my doctoral studies. I have a deep feeling of respect and appreciation for the message of the love of Christ that the Franciscans shared in the thirteenth, fourteen, and fifteenth centuries. Before I was hired full-time in Religious Education at BYU–Hawaii, I taught as a part-time faculty member of the history departments at both BYU and BYU–Hawaii. In that role I taught what felt like countless sections of the survey course The World to 1500, as well as courses on medieval history. As both a student and a teacher I have thought and taught about the world of the Middle Ages for many years.

Learning that I completed my PhD in religious studies, particularly with an emphasis on the history of Christianity, people often ask if it has affected my testimony. I have always been able to reply that my experiences have helped me to appreciate the Restoration more fully. The insights that I gained from my studies, my teaching, and my own reflections have opened up new insights into both the scriptures and the ordinances. Sometimes stepping back and seeing what we have in the Restoration with fresh eyes allows us to appreciate what we have had all along, but just have not been able to see because it was so familiar that it became invisible. Breaking out of a modern worldview, even briefly, can open us up to insights and perspectives that are embedded in the scriptures and ordinances. The medieval world can, in some ways, be a bridge back to ancient truths and insights. If nothing else, the differences from what we are familiar with can wake us up to see with fresh eyes. I hope that by looking through the lens of late medieval piety together I can share insights that will help you see the love of God manifest in the Restoration. The images of the scriptures, hymns, and ordinances can come alive and gain more power when we behold them and behold Christ in and through them.

In this part of the book, "Christ, Our Ransom Price," we will explore medieval images with an eye to how they can help us more clearly behold Christ in the scriptures and ordinances. We will start with some background on the role of devotional imagery and relics as a way to connect with the sacred and think about how images and physical connection with the holy are also part of our experience. We will then look at insights and skills of beholding that we can gain from particular types of devotional images: the *Arma Christi*, the imagery of Christ trampling the winepress, the Pietá, and the Man of Sorrows. This section then finishes with an exploration of the symbolism of the stigmata as a way to think about how one can be transformed into the image of Christ by beholding Christ and living a life of discipleship. The insights from medieval images can offer new ways of understanding sacred images and symbols. They provide us with ways to better behold and focus on Christ in covenants and worship. These images flesh out the spiritual understanding and changes that are embodied in coming to Christ through covenants and ordinances. The conclusion then brings together themes from both the ancient words and medieval images to help us see how connecting with Christ as the True Vine can bring greater joy and life to our journey on the covenant path.

CHAPTER 8

THE IMAGE OF CHRIST

In my exit interview with my mission president, he asked me what I had learned as a missionary. I told him that I had come to sense more fully Christ's power to bring things together that were falling apart. I talked about different experiences I had had and situations in which I had seen reconciliation and healing. I shared a passage at the end of section 6 of the Doctrine and Covenants that had helped me have confidence in Christ's power when everything seemed to be going wrong.

Christ's words had been a voice of comfort in hard experiences and times of disappointment: "Therefore, fear not, little flock; do good; let earth and hell combine against you, for if ye are built upon my rock, they cannot prevail. Behold, I do not condemn you; go your ways and sin no more; perform with soberness the work which I have commanded you" (Doctrine and Covenants 6:34–35). But more than just hearing that I was forgiven and encouraged to get up and get going again, what I had really learned from this section was that Christ's gift of the Atonement,

Christ invites us to behold the wounds and the prints of the nails so our faith and hope can grow. Geertgen tot Sint-Jans, Man van Smarten, *ca. 1490. Museum Catharijneconvent, Utrecht.*

his redeeming gift of ransom, stood behind every hope of things ever turning out right.

"Look unto me in every thought; doubt not, fear not. Behold the wounds which pierced my side, and also the prints of the nails in my hands and feet; be faithful, keep my commandments, and ye shall inherit the kingdom of heaven" (Doctrine and Covenants 6:36–37). In these verses I had found the constant when everything else—myself included—seemed fated to fall apart, over and over again. Christ pointed me to the source of faith and hope in every situation—looking to him and beholding his wounds.

When I was a child, my mother would encourage us to be quiet and reverent as they blessed and passed the sacrament. She told us we should think about the Savior. I tried to do that. I mostly found myself thinking about Jesus on a hillside surrounded by sheep. For a long time those pastoral scenes from Church artwork were the images that I had to meditate upon when I tried to remember the Savior.

If I had grown up in the later Middle Ages, it wouldn't have been so hard to behold Christ's side wound and the prints of the nails in his hands and feet. They were everywhere in late medieval piety. In addition to the many depictions in churches, woodblock prints spread images quickly in the era before the printing press. Working on my dissertation about the changes in Jerusalem pilgrimage in the context of late medieval passion piety, I looked at hundreds of images of Christ bleeding profusely. The wounds in his side, hands, and feet were all a source of great attention and love. Sometimes the wounds were exaggerated in the image for closer devotional reflection. Sometimes they were even separated from the body of Christ and displayed independently. There may have been a time when this devotional art was startling to me, but through my study, I could see the love that people felt for Christ reflected in these images.

We have many pictures of Christ in The Church of Jesus Christ of Latter-day Saints, and we are beginning to welcome a greater diversity of art styles into our religious artistic vocabulary. I'm glad that we're not iconoclastic, meaning that we don't reject images of Deity. Some religious traditions have interpreted the Ten Commandments in that way and don't allow pictures, or at least any pictures of God, to be created or displayed. Many branches of Islam produce primarily geometric art, and some Christian traditions, such as the Calvinist tradition, have had a focus on the word, not using religious images in churches for fear of idolatry.

Perhaps because there is such power in the visual, for believers there will always be some tension with images. One warning is to not make them the focus of our confidence. We see powerful corrections of idol worship in Old Testament prophetic writing. In very poetic terms, Isaiah reminds the people that when they go into captivity, they will be dragging their graven images with them. They will be a burden, not a source of help. "Bel boweth down, Nebo stoopeth, their idols were upon the beasts, and upon the cattle: your carriages were heavy loaden; they are a burden to the weary beast. They stoop, they bow down together; they could not deliver the burden, but themselves are gone into captivity" (Isaiah 46:1–2). The burden of carrying the images of the gods of Babylon is in direct contrast to the role of the true God of Israel, their Redeemer Jehovah. "Hearken unto me, O house of Jacob, and all the remnant of the house of Israel, which are borne by me from the belly, which are carried from the womb: And even to your old age I am he; and even to hoar hairs will I carry you: I have made, and I will bear; even I will carry, and will deliver you" (Isaiah 46:3–4). The Lord is there to carry us, not to be carried by us.

Again, I am grateful that we Latter-day Saints see religious art as an aid to faith and not as the source of our faith. Modern-day prophets have warned about idolatry. President Spencer W. Kimball's powerful 1976 article "The False Gods We Worship" comes to mind,[1] but the danger lies primarily in many other things in which we put our confidence. I'm grateful that we embrace the power of art, like the power of music, to lift our minds and hearts to worship and to contemplate the love and power of our Heavenly Father and his divine Son, Jesus Christ.

But, since we do use art, it helps to ponder briefly about how to use it in ways that can invite the Spirit of the Lord and increase our faith in

Christ. As we think more closely about devotional imagery, we can get insights into beholding Christ in the scriptures and the ordinances. While I focus here on medieval images, I am not advocating any particular style of imagery for our personal lives. My hope, instead, is that we can become aware of some things that we have in common with late medieval Christians and the role that devotional imagery played for them. This chapter focuses more generally on the use of devotional images as a witness of faith and a reminder of Christ; in later chapters we will be looking at more specific images and consider what we can learn from them in our effort to better behold Christ and more fully come unto him. Learning to see the images and symbols that point us to our Redeemer and his gift on our behalf increases our ability to behold our Father's message of hope.

Devotional Imagery

When I was a child I had a very small picture of Christ in a bright yellow plastic frame that I kept by my bedside. I think it was given to me by a Primary teacher. I liked having it there. I felt that it helped keep me safe in the dark. I think it reminded me that I was not alone but that the Savior was there for me. It was the famous greenish-toned, traditional image of Christ standing, knocking at the door. We Latter-day Saints also have a version of this image, with Christ in a red robe, but the one I had on my nightstand as a child was one that we have borrowed from our Protestant friends—it is widely beloved. In a contemporary world in which digital images can be shared, it has been interesting to see how images that originate in The Church of Jesus Christ of Latter-day Saints are also sometimes borrowed and used by Protestants.

In fact, having so many images that bring us together as Christians, we can hardly imagine a world in which images could be divisive, but that is part of what happened in the later Middle Ages and during the Reformation. The role of devotional images in the late medieval world as a sign or witness to others of faith is most sharply seen with the challenges of the Reformation in the sixteenth century. The iconoclastic, or anti-imagery, tendencies of several branches of the Reformation turned religious images into a visible symbol of allegiance.[2]

Almost everyone in Europe was Christian, but by then there were different kinds of Christians. As governments sought to impose their versions of Christianity, devotional images went up and came down as signs of loyalty or resistance to politically dominant churches.[3] One example of a religious image stashed away for future use is a nativity scene hidden under the church floor in Long Medford, England, during the reign of the Tudors—it was later "discovered unbroken under the church floor in the nineteenth century."[4] During the reigns of Henry, Edward, Mary, and Elizabeth, the English experienced many different versions of religious worship and dramatically different roles of devotional art. The faithful people in Long Medford wanted to preserve a scene at a time when it was not welcome, in hopes that the prevailing mood would shift and they could bring it out and celebrate the birth of Christ again with this representation of the stable of Bethlehem.

Like late medieval Christians, we members of Christ's Church love nativity sets. Many of our congregations have open houses during the Christmas season to which we invite neighbors to view many kinds of Christmas crèches from around the world and to celebrate the birth of Christ with us. Religious images are a means by which we show our religious allegiance and faith in Christ. This role of religious images as a sign of our faith and commitment can be seen in a story told by Virginia U. Jensen, a former first counselor in the Relief Society General Presidency. A little girl was lost, but upon entering the home of a couple that offered to help her find her parents, she saw a picture of the Savior. The girl commented, "I was frightened until I saw the picture of Jesus hanging on your wall. Then I knew I would be safe."[5] We feel safe with these images of the Savior, and we want others to feel safe in his Church with images that they also love and cherish.

Having pictures of Christ in our churches and homes is a witness to others of our faith in him. President Ezra Taft Benson described the disciples of Christ: "Enter their homes, and the pictures on their walls, the books on their shelves, the music in the air, their words and acts reveal them as Christians."[6] Devotional images can signal our beliefs and priorities to others and thereby invite them to be followers themselves.

Another aspect of the late medieval use of devotional images that can resonate with us is using images to remember. Surrounding ourselves with images of Christ not only signals our faith to others but can also serve as a reminder to ourselves. Late medieval piety centered on Christ's suffering and death on behalf of humankind. Through the widespread and often graphic images of Christ's suffering, people sought to remember and to more fully understand the extent of that suffering. They knew that Christ's suffering and death were the means by which they had a hope of being free from their sins and being reconciled with God, and they sought to keep that awareness before them.

The forms of imagery that they used are often unfamiliar to us. We do not use crucifixes to remember his atoning death, and our popular images of Christ rarely depict his suffering on our behalf, but faith in his Atonement is likewise central to our faith. We have covenanted to always remember him, and devotional art can help us to always remember.

Just as the role of Christ was central to the faith of late medieval Christians, so it is with us. Likewise, the representation of Christ is something that we can think about seriously. The very foreignness of the distant mirror of late medieval piety can help us appreciate the importance of looking to Christ and not merely to a representation of Christ. Looking to Christ is the source of our salvation. Just as the children of Israel looked upon the type of the brazen serpent and lived, so we are invited to "cast about [our] eyes and begin to believe in the Son of God, that he will come to redeem his people, and that he shall suffer and die to atone for their sins" (Alma 33:22; see 33:18–23). Only by looking to our Redeemer and the ransom price of his atoning sacrifice can we find eternal life.

As we think about the role of images, we recognize that images can help us remember to look, but we must not look only to images. Images cannot be the source of a relationship or connection with the Savior.

Images alone cannot be a source of emotional reassurance and protection. Images cannot provide an assurance that Christ is real.

Thinking about the role of devotional imagery reminds us of the importance of having a spiritual relationship with a Being rather than an emotional relationship with an image. Familiar images can appropriately provide a source of emotional comfort, but we should not mistake the emotional reassurance of a familiar image with a spiritual experience. Having images of Christ cannot and must not be a substitute for looking to Christ. Images can, however, point us to the Being to whom we can look. They can help us to always remember him and the price he paid for our redemption.

When life is hard and painful, remembering Christ can pull us out of the discouragement that we can easily sink into. Consider Mormon's words to his son Moroni after describing the depravity of his people: "May not the things which I have written grieve thee, to weigh thee down unto death; but may Christ lift thee up, and may his sufferings and death, and the showing his body unto our fathers, and his mercy and long-suffering, and the hope of his glory and of eternal life, rest in your mind forever" (Moroni 9:25). Beholding his ransom price reminds us that we are free and we can live with joy and peace even in a fallen and wicked world. Christ's "sufferings and death, and the showing his body" are the images of late medieval passion piety, and they are the symbols of the ordinances. He invites us to "behold the wounds which pierced my side, and also the prints of the nails in my hands and feet" (Doctrine and Covenants 6:37). Beholding his wounds, in both his mortal and resurrected body, allows us to behold that he has truly paid the price and won the victory. When we let this rest in our minds forever, we can more fully have "the hope of his glory and of eternal life."

Notes

1. Spencer W. Kimball, "The False Gods We Worship," *Ensign*, June 1976, 2–6.

2. The followers of Zwingli and Calvin are most noted for their iconoclastic positions. Lutheran practice was generally more accepting of visual images. See Carl C. Christensen, *Art and Reformation in Germany* (Athens: Ohio University Press, 1979); and Robert W. Scribner, *For the Sake of Simple Folk: Popular Propaganda for the German Reformation* (Cambridge: Cambridge University Press, 1981).

3. This is most strikingly illustrated in the English Reformations. The dramatic back and forth religious changes were matched by changes in church and home visual imagery. See, for example, Eamon Duffy, *The Stripping of the Altars: Traditional Religion in England, 1400–1580* (New Haven, CT: Yale University Press, 1992), 421–22, 431, 439, 451, 478–503.

4. Duffy, *Stripping of the Altars*, 490.

5. Virginia U. Jensen, "Home, Family, and Personal Enrichment," *Ensign*, November 1999, 97.

6. Ezra Taft Benson, *A Witness and a Warning: A Modern Day Prophet Testifies of the Book of Mormon* (Salt Lake City: Deseret Book, 1988), 65; see Benson, "Born of God," *Ensign*, July 1989, 5.

Procession of relics. The remains of the saints were seen as a means of access to holiness and God's power. Jean Pucelle, The Hours of Jeanne d'Evreux, Queen of France, *fol. 173v, detail, ca. 1324–28. The Metropolitan Museum of Art, New York, The Cloisters Collection, 1954. www.metmuseum.org (CC0 1.0).*

CHAPTER 9

RELICS

My mother passed away when I was thirty-four, and she was buried in a peaceful cemetery overlooking Provo, Utah. I don't live in Utah, but when I come to visit family I also go to say hi to Mom. I know that her spirit may be elsewhere, busy in the work of the spirit world, but her gravesite is where her body is buried, and so she is still there in a sense. Walking over to her tombstone and saying hi, telling her that I love her, gives a sense of connection and anticipation of the resurrection. I know that I will see her again, that her spirit and body will be reunited, and that I will be able to give her a hug. In the meantime, it's nice to have a feeling of connection.

In the early days of Christianity, after the era when Christians were martyred but while that memory was still fresh, Christians would go to the graves of the martyrs.[1] They believed in the bodily resurrection, but they knew that while their bodies waited in the ground, the spirits of the martyrs were alive in the presence of God. They sought out a relationship with those martyred saints by being close to them. They wanted to take those saints as a patron, much like patrons in the Roman world of late antiquity in which they lived. In the Roman world, wealthy and powerful people were patrons who had clients that depended on them. By taking care of their clients, the patrons showed their power and, in return, the clients would praise and honor their patron.

The early Christians who took these saints as patrons believed that those saints would put in a good word for them with God and Christ, who were more powerful but seemed less accessible. The Christians had faith that God and Christ could be approached by the saintly martyrs whose spirits were in their presence. These early Christians believed that by going to the martyrs' tombs they would be in the presence of the saints' physical bodies. The saints' physical remains provided a means of contact with beings in the presence of God. In time, the saints' remains became more mobile. Through relics, the physical remains of the saints, along with their holiness, could be moved to other sites and thereby become accessible for more people.[2] Even divided, a part of the saint's body represented the whole. The early saints were understood to be present in these relics. The relics were a physical means by which people could feel close to a holy being that was not only there with them but was also in the presence of God.

Relics throughout Europe

Relics became even more important as the early Middle Ages moved toward the central Middle Ages—it became a requirement that churches be built on the site of a martyr's body. As Christianity spread further north, beyond the range of the early martyrs, the movement of relics was essential to spread the holiness they were believed to embody. Having the remains of the martyr meant that the saint was present. The presence of the saint brought the individuals who worshipped there closer to the presence of God. For example, the cathedrals built in the central Middle

Ages had relics as part of their foundation, typically beneath the high altar.

These cathedrals represent a time of greater urbanization and trade. As cities became larger, the people wanted to make statements about the importance of their cities, as well as showing their devotion by having the biggest and best architecture. As a missionary I served in two cities that had been important in medieval France and often biked past these magnificent structures. Saint-Étienne Cathedral in Limoges was a soaring Gothic church, and Saint-Front in Périgueux was a remarkable multi-domed building, which, I learned later, was modeled after St. Mark's in Venice. Hundreds of years after their heyday, these cathedrals continued to portray the faith of their era. They were not places where I went to worship, nor were they for many others, but it was clear that they had been the central point of their respective cities when they were built.

Not everyone lived in large cities or towns, but these churches had a broader influence. In addition to having a relic under the high altar, displaying relics for pilgrims also became an important draw for churches. Relics were placed in reliquaries that were sometimes designed like miniature gold- and gem-encrusted caskets or churches; they also sometimes depicted the shape of an arm or a head. People longed to be in contact with the holiness represented by these saints, and many traveled long distances to churches with relics.

In this world of great cathedrals and monasteries, the clergy were divided into two groups, religious and secular. The monks and nuns were called the "religious." Ordinary people as well as nobles essentially delegated the responsibility of being holy to the monks. Their canonical hours of prayers allowed the blessings of God to be poured out on nearby towns and the noble families that supported them. The "secular" clergy, the priests and bishops who were out in the world (thus earning the term *secular*), were also important. They helped with the sacraments that were seen as necessary for salvation, but the monasteries had a privileged place as the site of learning and study. Local priests were often very poorly educated.

In the monasteries, as monks studied and copied sacred texts, there arose some important concepts that changed the European religious world. The focus on Christ gradually moved away from the perception of a distant divinity, removed from human experience and sympathy that had required the saints to act as patrons. Instead, the focus on the humanity of Christ as the source of salvation grew. This devotion to Christ's mortal life led to new ways of thinking about salvation.[3]

The earlier medieval depiction of Christ as the stern and terrifying judge at the last day helped explain the need for patron saints to put in a good word for us. In this new monastic focus, there was instead a greater appreciation of Christ himself being our intercessor through his own suffering and blood. This later focus on the humanity, or physical aspect, of Christ emphasized his suffering as a substitute for our suffering. This can be seen in St. Anselm's (1033/34–1109) theological treatise *Why God Became Man* and Bernard of Clairvaux's (1090–1153) meditations on the love of God seen in the suffering and death of Christ that we know from the hymn with his words, "Jesus the very thought of thee with sweetness fills my breast; but sweeter far thy face to see and in thy presence rest."[4]

During this later medieval period we start to see many more images of the suffering

Relics provided a material connection to the presence of holy beings whose spirits were with God. Arm reliquary, ca. 1230. The Metropolitan Museum of Art, New York, The Cloisters Collection, 1947.

Christ in art as a way to show God's love. We also see the rise of devotion to Mary. It was understood that through her, Christ became human and received his physical body.[5] His flesh was her flesh. The experience of communion, or Eucharist, meaning the sacrament of the Lord's Supper, also became much more important because it was a way to connect with the body of Christ. During this era we see development of the ideas of the real presence and doctrine of transubstantiation, which emphasized that with the consecration by the priest, the bread and wine maintained the appearance of bread and wine but became Christ's body and blood in a way that could not be seen. Holiness was found in Christ's body, in his incarnation, not just in the bodies of the saints. One example of this can be seen in which the holiness of a consecrated host, the wafer or bread of the sacrament, came to be seen as a replacement for a relic in the consecration of the church.

While many of these specific doctrines are not ones that we hold as members of The Church of Jesus Christ of Latter-day Saints, I can see the Spirit of the Lord working on a people and moving their hearts and minds toward a love of Christ and a confidence in his atoning suffering and death. The devotional practices of that era reflect an extremely deep appreciation and gratitude for the love of God manifest in the suffering and death of Christ. This is what we call passion piety, devotion focused on his *passio* or suffering. This is where we start to see all the images of Christ suffering and bleeding. A focus on Christ's passion means a focus on Christ's suffering. Medieval religious meditations on the suffering and death of Christ didn't deny the reality of the Resurrection but were instead expressions of gratitude that we could be saved in and through the atoning blood of Jesus Christ.

Into this world of increasing focus on Christ as the source of salvation came the Franciscan and Dominican movements in the 1200s, the thirteenth century. Earlier in the Middle Ages, Benedictine monks in the monasteries often became very wealthy because of the donations made to them by wealthy people seeking for blessings; but then, as the monks' lives became more comfortable, people sometimes wondered if this comfort

FINDING CHRIST IN THE COVENANT PATH

Later in the Middle Ages emphasis was shifted to encountering the presence of Christ through passion relics or the consecrated host (sacrament bread), which was often displayed for viewing in a transparent receptacle known as a monstrance. Sacrament cupboard door, fifteenth century. Museum Schnütgen, Köln.

kept them from living lives that allowed them to properly intercede and pray on their behalf. There were various monastic reform movements, but the tendency to slip into a luxurious lifestyle kept recurring.

The Franciscans and Dominicans were new kinds of monks: poor monks. They were called mendicants, which means "beggar." They didn't stay cloistered in monasteries praying but traveled and taught people in towns, getting them excited about the message of Christ's sacrifice and love and encouraging them to live lives of holiness. One example of this encouragement to holiness is found in a fourteenth-century religious text influenced by Franciscan piety called the *Vita Christi* or *Life of Christ*: "We ought to carry the Cross of our Lord and help Him to bear it, with our hearts by pious remembrance and compassion, with our lips by frequent and devout thanksgiving, with our whole body by mortification and penance, and thus give thanks to our Saviour by our affections, words and deeds."[6] The mendicants showed and taught that one's whole being needed to be an expression of love for God and gratitude for the gift of his Son.

Passion Relics

Throughout the Middle Ages, pilgrims had traveled to Jerusalem, but with the rise of the Crusades in the eleventh and twelfth centuries, a greater number of Europeans traveled to the Holy Land. In fact, the increased exposure to the physical realities of Christ's mortal experience is believed to have factored into the shift in theology toward a meditation on the human dimension of Christ's life, suffering, and death. Pilgrims and crusaders brought back not just descriptions of the holy sites of Jerusalem but also physical remnants that connected people with the life of the Savior—things like stones, earth, or objects associated with the birth or the passion of Christ, such as fragments of the cross, sponge, nails, spear, and so forth. So, just as physical remnants of the holy saints and martyrs of early Christianity had been a source of access and power for many centuries, in the later Middle Ages, physical connections to the life and death of the Son of God became treasured as passion relics.

Some of these objects had already been preserved and treasured by Eastern Christians in Constantinople and other sites, but many of

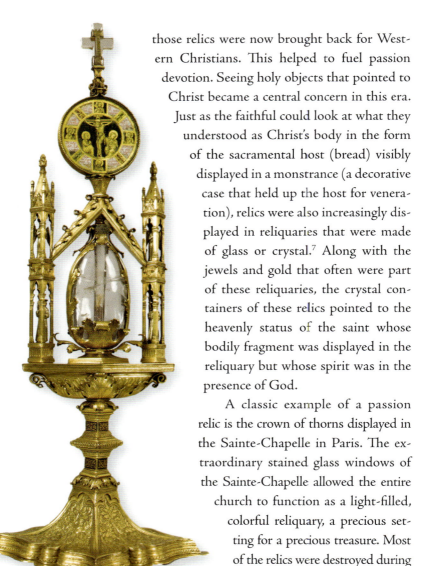

those relics were now brought back for Western Christians. This helped to fuel passion devotion. Seeing holy objects that pointed to Christ became a central concern in this era. Just as the faithful could look at what they understood as Christ's body in the form of the sacramental host (bread) visibly displayed in a monstrance (a decorative case that held up the host for veneration), relics were also increasingly displayed in reliquaries that were made of glass or crystal.[7] Along with the jewels and gold that often were part of these reliquaries, the crystal containers of these relics pointed to the heavenly status of the saint whose bodily fragment was displayed in the reliquary but whose spirit was in the presence of God.

A classic example of a passion relic is the crown of thorns displayed in the Sainte-Chapelle in Paris. The extraordinary stained glass windows of the Sainte-Chapelle allowed the entire church to function as a light-filled, colorful reliquary, a precious setting for a precious treasure. Most of the relics were destroyed during the French Revolution, but the

Crystal and gold reliquaries pointed to the spirit of the saint dwelling in heaven. Reliquary of Mary Magdalene, fourteenth and fifteenth centuries. The Metropolitan Museum of Art, New York, Gift of J. Pierpont Morgan, 1917.

church remains as a premier example of Gothic architecture. The king of France showed his devotion to Christ by obtaining passion relics from Constantinople around 1240. In 1248 the amazing church of the Sainte-Chapelle was consecrated as a place for the French kings to hold their greatest treasure, the crown of thorns. In addition to this premier relic of passion piety, the church's collection included other objects associated with Christ's suffering, including fragments of the lance (spear), sponge, cross, and burial shroud.[8] We see here the continuity of relic devotion from the early Christian period but with a shift to passion piety, the focus on Christ's suffering and death.

What can we make of this as Latter-day Saints? Like the Protestants of the Reformation, it is easy to scoff at the number of fragments of the True Cross that are reported to be housed in churches and reliquaries throughout Europe. We are better served, however, if we think about what these tangible connections with the life of Christ were doing for them and what role physical connection with the past and with holiness has for us.

Relics and History

In the Sacred Grove there are some trees that are very old. They are known as "witness trees." They were around during the appearance of the Father and the Son to Joseph Smith in 1820. If all the trees that had been alive at that time had died, it would not change what happened. If the entire grove burned down and was covered over with pavement, it would not change what happened. The trees aren't essential to connect with sacred history, but there is still something powerful and awe-inspiring about being able to walk through that bit of forest. I grew up in Virginia and have walked in many Eastern forests with towering trees and forest undergrowth, but there is something special about being in Palmyra and thinking, "This is the place. This is the place where God revealed himself and introduced his Beloved Son."

Physical connections with the past bring memories. We go back to our childhood home, and we see, smell, and hear what we experienced in our youth. We know we are not in the past, but the past seems closer, and place brings it to mind in a fuller, more experiential way. These memories might be happy or sad, but being in a specific place or touching something from that place offers a bridge to what was.

While place is not transportable, matter is. I can be anywhere and open a box of my mission letters from France or a box of my father's mission letters from Germany or the record book from my grandfather's mission in England, and a bridge to that past experience opens up. Not even reading them, but just experiencing the physical presence of these records is powerful. The stamps and special airmail envelopes speak of an era of distance and slower communication. They speak of faith and devotion to live in a foreign land to share the message of the gospel of Jesus Christ. Keeping family records, heirlooms, and momentos can be a powerful way to bring the past to mind, to make the experience of others real to us today.

As a church, we put an emphasis on Church history as well as on family history. There are many beautifully preserved and restored Church history sites. We can essentially go on pilgrimage to feel a connection with the events in Palmyra, New York; Kirtland, Ohio; Independence, Missouri; and Nauvoo and Carthage, Illinois. For those who are not able to travel to those sites, the Church produces beautiful films recounting the history and sharing the visual experiences of being in those sacred places. If we do get to travel, we can bring back physical reminders of the places for ourselves or to share with friends. Just as I have little clay oil lamps from a trip to Jerusalem, I also have a replica copy of the first edition Book of Mormon from Palmyra that I can handle and show others. I have little red bricks from Nauvoo, bringing to mind the Red Brick Store where the Relief Society was organized and the temple endowment was first administered. We don't believe these physical reminders bring salvation, but we don't shun them in hopes of having a purely spiritual and nonmaterial connection with God and sacred history.

Tangible Connection with Christ

Where then do we find the physical that points to salvation? Where do we find the connection with Christ's suffering and death that people honored in their reverence for remnants of the cross, the nails, the spear, the sponge, the crown of thorns, or the cloth that wiped Christ's forehead? In the later Middle Ages, even a tiny scrap of any of these sacred passion relics was sufficient to justify building a monumental church, starting a special feast day, or setting out on a long pilgrimage to make a connection with a piece of something that had been there with Christ. The idea that some physical remnant could bring his presence closer brought great joy and devotion. People traveled for many miles to see or touch something that the Savior had touched.

There is a parable in Matthew 24 that I love to explore with my classes. It sounds a little disturbing and sinister at first. "For wheresoever the carcase is, there will the eagles be gathered together" (24:28). I ask who has seen eagles or vultures flying in circles. People know that this circling means these scavengers have found something dead to eat. These birds get life from the death of other animals. Then we look at the Joseph Smith Translation in the Pearl of Great Price. "And now I show unto you a parable. Behold, wheresoever the carcass is, there will the eagles be gathered together; so likewise shall mine elect be gathered from the four quarters of the earth" (Joseph Smith—Matthew 1:27). We then talk about where we gather as Saints in all the quarters of the earth and what we gather for. This gathering is a sign of the last days and points to what is now available through the restoration of priesthood keys.

We gather together for sacrament meetings. We gather together in temples. We gather together because that is where we are nourished. That is where we find life through the death of the Son of God. This is why we are gathered. I don't think it is a coincidence that the white cloth covering the emblems of the sacrament looks like a burial shroud.

Christ said, "This is my body" and "This is my blood." He also said, "Take, eat" and "Drink ye all of it" (Matthew 26:26–28). We don't have to develop any kind of elaborate theory of real presence or transubstantiation to make sense of what he is trying to tell us. Even though the bread and water are offered to us, we have to reach out and take the emblems for ourselves. We put the bread and water into our mouths. Christ wants to be present for us and in us, and we can choose to receive what he is offering. He wants to connect with us and allow us to connect with him. He wants to lift us in the most physically elemental way that we know, by feeding us and quenching our thirst.

When I read the Gospel of John with students, we talk about how long we can live without food and how long we can live without water. We all know that we are completely dependent on outside substances to maintain our life. The Gospel of John teaches that Christ has come to be the bread of life and the living water. Christ wants us to connect with him through his Spirit, but he also provides a physical, tactile way for us to encounter his suffering and death. He wants what he experienced to be real for us. As we partake of broken bread we can ponder the hymn: "Bruised, broken, torn for us on Calvary's hill—thy suffering borne for us lives with us still."[9]

In the suffering and death of Christ, we find the love of God that feeds the deepest hunger of our souls. He invites us to come unto him, just as he did to the multitude at the temple in Bountiful after his resurrection. In our sacrament meetings, he wants us to be able to touch and taste the love that he has for us. In the ordinances of the temple, he also offers us a way to feel and touch the love that he has for us. He wants the historical reality of his suffering and death to be present for us. The ordinances allow us to bridge the historical distance. They connect us with the reality of his atoning sacrifice and redeeming love.

Notes

1. The classic discussion of this topic is Peter Brown, *The Cult of the Saints: Its Rise and Function in Latin Christianity* (Chicago: University of Chicago Press, 1982).

2. The classic study of the movement of relics is Patrick J. Geary, *Furta Sacra: Thefts of Relics in the Middle Ages*, rev. ed. (Princeton, NJ: Princeton University Press, 1991).

3. An early Christian framework to think about salvation, known as the *Christus Victor* theory, had portrayed human salvation as a divine victory over death and hell. In this way of thinking, the devil thought he had won by having Christ killed but then found that he could not keep the divine Christ in hell as he broke out, bringing others with him.

4. Bernard of Clairvaux, "Jesus, the Very Thought of Thee," trans. Edward Caswall, in *Hymns* (Salt Lake City: The Church of Jesus Christ of Latter-day Saints, 1985), no. 141.

5. Caroline Walker Bynum gives an important discussion of the understanding of Christ's flesh as Mary's flesh in *Holy Feast, Holy Fast: The Religious Significance of Food to Medieval Women* (Berkeley: University of California Press, 1998).

6. Ludolph of Saxony. *Vita Christi*. Selections found in *The Hours of the Passion Taken from "The Life of Christ" by Ludoph the Saxon*, ed. Henry J. Coleridge (London: Burns and Oates, 1887), 7; emphasis added.

7. An excellent discussion of reliquaries and their different forms throughout Christian history can be found in Cynthia Hahn, *The Reliquary Effect: Enshrining the Sacred Object* (London: Reaktion Books, 2017).

8. Daniel Weiss, *Art and Crusade in the Age of Saint Louis* (Cambridge: Cambridge University Press, 1998), 221n15.

9. Hugh W. Dougall, "Jesus of Nazareth, Savior and King," in *Hymns*, no. 181.

Christ with the crown of thorns. Devotional images of Christ's suffering helped viewers remember and feel his redeeming love. Petrus Christus, Head of Christ, ca. 1445. The Metropolitan Museum of Art, New York, Bequest of Lillian S. Timken, 1959.

CHAPTER 10

ARMA CHRISTI

Many years ago, I had an experience in which I was the target of an unexpected outburst of anger and derision. The effect on my soul and emotions was crushing. This eruption of anger directed toward me left me wounded and in pain. After enduring the tongue-lashing, I had a chance to go into a restroom to dry my tears and compose myself. There I had a sobering but uplifting experience. As I looked into the bathroom mirror, what my mind saw reflected was an image of Christ wearing a crown of thorns. I know that remembering the Savior's suffering in our times of suffering can sometimes remind us of the message found in Doctrine and Covenants 122:8, that he has suffered more than we will ever have to go through. At that moment, however, the message that I felt was that he had felt and was feeling my pain. "Surely he hath borne our griefs, and carried our sorrows" (Isaiah 53:4). His sorrow helped to lift my sorrow.

In late medieval piety, sometimes the image of the suffering Christ was accompanied with the text from Lamentations: "Behold, and see if there be any sorrow like unto my sorrow" (1:12). The pervasive late medieval efforts to meditate on the suffering of Christ was not a negation of his glorious resurrection. Their belief in a bodily resurrection was a source of hope, as believers had confidence that through him they would also be raised up. Nevertheless, during mortality, through the pains and griefs that we endure, both physical and spiritual, looking to the wounds and pain of Christ can be a focus of meditation that brings comfort and healing.

Part of the structure of this meditation in the later Middle Ages was offered through the presentation of the story of Christ's passion, his suffering and death. A particularly focused means of meditation was often made available in visually condensed images known as the *Arma Christi*. With these images, one item represented one scene of the biblical passion account. Seeing a picture of a glove or gauntlet brought to mind Christ being struck on the face during his questioning at the trial. Seeing a picture of a whip or a cat o' nine tails brought to mind Christ's scourging. Seeing an image of the nails brought to mind his body crucified on the cross. These images, collected together to focus the mind on Christ's suffering, were called the *Arma Christi* because they portrayed the arms or weapons of Christ, meaning the weapons that were used against him in his passion, but also indicating that these instruments of his suffering were his arms in the sense of heraldry and also his weapons in his victory over Satan.

In the presentation of the *Arma Christi*, specificity is important. These images are not a general meditation on the general suffering of Christ. The *Arma Christi* present specific images to aid in remembrance and meditation: the silver coins representing the price paid to betray him, the rooster or cock that crowed when Peter denied knowing him, a face that spat upon him, the crown of thorns with which he was mocked, the nails, the sponge with which he was offered vinegar, the spear that pierced his side, the ladder from which he was taken down from the cross. The

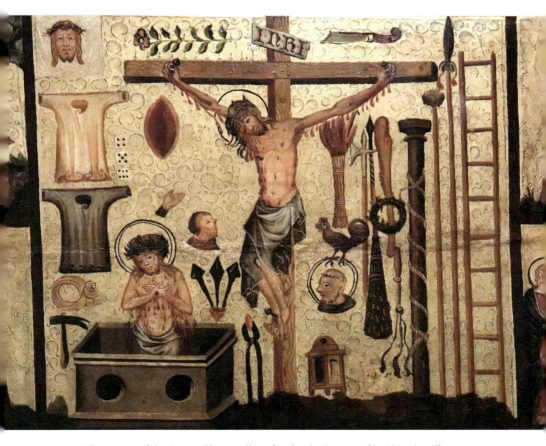

The images of the Arma Christi allowed individuals to ponder Christ's suffering and love. Scenes from Divine Plan of Salvation, detail, around 1370–80. Wallraf-Richartz-Museum, Köln.

Arma Christi were not, however, presented in a narrative, chronological way. They also were not detailed representations but sketches of the items. They were almost like what we would look for today in clip art representations.

This lack of detail was actually connected to the role these images played in communication.[1] The *Arma Christi* functioned as signs that pointed to what was real. They weren't trying to be the object itself.

In *De doctrina Christiana* Augustine described a sign as "a thing which causes us to think of something beyond the impression the thing itself makes upon our senses."[2] The signifier, the reality to which each sign pointed, was a particular event of Christ's atoning suffering and death. These signs allowed focused, particular meditation, but seen altogether, they also pointed toward the totality of Christ's passion.

Part of the focus of the *Arma Christi* was on what Christ suffered; these were the weapons used against him. These images of weapons, however, also reflected Christ not just as a victim but also as a victor. Christ's suffering and death, made possible through these physical items, were his victory over death and hell. Many images show the Risen Christ, in glory, surrounded by angels that carry the *Arma Christi*. He won the victory with his suffering and death. It was not a defeat but instead a glorious triumph that he gained through his willingness to suffer and die on our behalf. The *Arma Christi* represented, in a sense, the victory that we have through him. As Isaiah prophesied: "He was wounded for our transgressions, he was bruised for our iniquities: the chastisement of our peace was upon him; and with his stripes we are healed" (Isaiah 53:5).

Pondering the Passion

As Latter-day Saints, we sometimes hesitate to spend time in meditation on the suffering of Christ, knowing with additional certainty the reality of the glorious Risen Lord through the revelations in the latter days. I would suggest that one way to increase our faith in his redeeming power is by taking time to consider the redemption price paid for us. In the Doctrine and Covenants, we are told to "listen to him who is the advocate with the Father" and "who is pleading your cause before him" (45:3). When we recognize how much we need mercy and when we listen to the Savior speaking as our advocate, our gratitude and love for him increase.

As we listen to our advocate, we notice what he points out to the Father. Are these things that we should behold as well? "Father, behold the sufferings and death of him who did no sin, in whom thou wast well pleased; behold the blood of thy Son which was shed, the blood of him whom thou gavest that thyself might be glorified" (Doctrine and Covenants 45:4). "*Behold* the sufferings and death of him who did no sin." If Christ's suffering and death are just an abstraction or an idea for us, it is hard for his atoning sacrifice to soften our hearts. Taking time to behold his sufferings and death opens our heart and mind to the love he had for us in order to suffer and die on our behalf. To the extent that Christ's suffering and death remain merely a puzzle piece fitting in with all the pieces in the plan of salvation, we are not able to hear his pleading on our behalf or behold his love. Taking the time to behold the blood that he shed for us can move our hearts to a response of love and gratitude

Many of our sacrament hymns also invite us into this immediate, personal reflection on the blood shed for us. One hymn in particular evokes the same feeling that the Savior's words do in section 45 of the Doctrine and Covenants.

> Rev'rently and meekly now,
> Let thy head most humbly bow
> Think of me, thou ransomed one;
> Think what I for thee have done.
> With my blood that dripped like rain,
> Sweat in agony of pain,
> With my body on the tree
> I have ransomed even thee.[3]

The first person language of the hymn allows us to hear the Savior's invitation in our own voices as we sing and thus makes the Redeemer's gift of his suffering and death personal and immediate. He did this for me. He has ransomed even me.

In Doctrine and Covenants 45, the Savior explains the reason that the Father should behold the blood of Christ: "Wherefore, Father, spare these my brethren that believe on my name, that they may come unto me and have everlasting life" (45:5). I don't think that the Father needs persuading to spare us. The plan of redemption is his plan. He already knows the power of the redeeming blood of Christ. Instead, I think we are the ones that need persuading to believe that we can be spared. We need persuading that we can come unto him and have everlasting life.

Christ invites us to behold, to pay serious and concerted attention to his redeeming blood so that we can more fully "believe on his name" (Doctrine and Covenants 45:5). Our faith that we can "come unto [him] and have everlasting life" (45:5) will be directly connected to our ability to "behold the sufferings and death of him who did no sin." To trust that we have been redeemed, we must "behold the blood of [God's] Son which was shed, the blood of him whom [God gave that he] might be glorified" (45:4). God the Father gave us his Son. The Son gave us his life, his sufferings, and his death.

Slowing Down

Taking time to behold Christ's suffering and death is not a "to do" item on a checklist of spiritual responsibilities. Beholding Christ's suffering and death keeps the redemption alive for us. It keeps his love and ransom price real for us. I am not advocating that we plaster our walls with endless visual depictions of Christ's passion, but I believe that we can develop habits of mind and heart as we practice slowing down to "behold the sufferings and death of him who did no sin" (Doctrine and Covenants 45:5). The individual images and symbols of the *Arma Christi* provide one strategy for meditation and pondering. They show us a way to behold. There is value in slowing down and separating the images of his suffering and death rather than lumping them all together under the umbrella of the Atonement. There is value in looking at the signs with an eye to understand the reality that is signified by them.

Early in the Book of Mormon, we see Nephi's serious reflection on the future sufferings of Christ that he has learned about from the prophets. Nephi's meditation has an additional level of soberness because he is reflecting not only on what Christ will suffer but also on a universal human response to him. Isaiah 53 has a similar way of bringing us into the story of Christ's suffering. Christ is not portrayed at a distance from us, with other people doing bad things to him. Instead, Isaiah implicates all of us in Christ's suffering: "He is despised and rejected of men; a man of sorrows, and acquainted with grief: and *we* hid as it were *our* faces from him; he was despised, and *we* esteemed him not" (Isaiah 53:3; emphasis added).

Nephi begins his meditation by considering that the way we treat the words of Christ is, in a sense, the way we treat him. "For the things which some men esteem to be of great worth, both to the body and soul, others set at naught and trample under their feet. Yea, even the very God of Israel do men trample under their feet; I say, trample under their feet but I would speak in other words—they set him at naught, and hearken not to the voice of his counsels" (1 Nephi 19:7). Nephi introduces and then moves away from the direct comparison of disregarding him and his word to trampling Christ, the God of Israel, underfoot. Still, he has introduced that image—that we can trample him under our feet with our response to him.

Nephi next focuses on how Christ will be treated during his suffering and death. Note that, like Isaiah, Nephi's emphasis is not on the historical response to Christ, but on a more general, universal human response. It is "the world" that rejects him and considers him as "a thing of naught." "And behold he cometh, according to the words of the angel, in six hundred years from the time my father left Jerusalem. And the world, because of their iniquity, shall judge him to be a thing of naught; wherefore they scourge him, and he suffereth it; and they smite him, and he suffereth it. Yea, they spit upon him, and he suffereth it, because of his loving kindness and his long-suffering towards the children of men" (1 Nephi 19:8–9).

Nephi doesn't focus on the historical actors, the people who lived at the time of Jesus. Instead, he depicts Christ's submission to mistreatment as an expression of his patience and compassion toward all of us. He endures this suffering because of "his loving kindness and his long-suffering towards the children of men." We are all implicated in what he suffers.

Note that in this meditation Nephi goes through the different actions one by one: "they *scourge him*, and he suffereth it"; and "they *smite him*, and he suffereth it"; and "they *spit upon him*, and he suffereth it." Each particular and specific action emphasizes the particular pain and humiliation associated with this suffering and abuse that he permitted to occur.

Emphasizing Christ's sufferings as well as his death often leads us to focus exclusively on Gethsemane, but Nephi's meditation expands our view to the suffering between Gethsemane and the cross. His step-by-step examination of Christ's sufferings can be similar to the meditation on the *Arma Christi*. When we slow down to ponder them, we can see in each particular step of Christ's suffering a manifestation of his love for us. Isaiah gave a similar witness of why thinking about this suffering can matter for us: "But he was wounded for our transgressions, he was bruised for our iniquities: the chastisement of our peace was upon him; and with his stripes we are healed" (Isaiah 53:5), or "the punishment that brought us peace was upon him, and by his wounds [or welts] we are healed" (New International Version, Isaiah 53:5). As we slow down to consider the accounts of Christ's suffering we can know more fully that he was wounded, bruised, and beaten for us. Slowing down to remember and ponder his stripes can give us additional confidence that we can be healed.

Receiving the Atonement

I received my mission call to France during the summer, but I wasn't assigned to report to the MTC until after Thanksgiving. During that time, I worked as a waitress and spent much of my free time reading the Book of Mormon, studying French, and listening to Handel's *Messiah*. I was fortunate to be able to receive my endowment several months before I began my mission, and I attended the temple every week. One of my clearest memories is actually of my first time through the temple while receiving my own endowment. There was a lot of symbolism to take in, and the part of my mind that uses words didn't process everything. But there is another part of my mind that uses music, and as I went through the session I heard arias from the *Messiah*. By the time I arrived in the celestial room the one thing I knew for sure was that the endowment was about Christ and his Atonement.

Elder Bruce C. Hafen and Sister Marie K. Hafen have thoughtfully observed that in the Gospels we read the story of Christ performing the Atonement and in the endowment, we experience the story of Adam and Eve receiving the Atonement.[4] Slowing down to think about the images and signs that point toward Christ's suffering is a powerful tool. As we read and ponder scriptures and as we attend the temple, we can see symbols and signs representing what Christ suffered for us in giving us the gift of the Atonement. Learning to ponder on these signs can help us develop capacities for meditation and reflection in considering the signs and symbols through which we receive that gift. Learning to see Christ's suffering and death as a process can help us see that our receiving the gift of the Savior's Atonement is also a process. It doesn't all happen at once. There are steps and stages to the process. The gift of Christ's ransom price can have a transformative power as we more clearly behold and receive what we are being offered.

Notes

1. See Heather Madar, "Iconography of Sign: A Semiotic Reading of the Arma Christi," in *Revisioning: Critical Methods of Seeing Christianity in the History of Art*, ed. James Romaine and Linda Stratford, Art for Faith's Sake Series (Eugene, OR: Cascade Books, 2013), 115–32.

2. Augustine, *On Christian Doctrine* 2.1.

3. Joseph L. Townsend, "Reverently and Meekly Now," in *Hymns* (Salt Lake City: The Church of Jesus Christ of Latter-day Saints, 1985), no. 185.

4. Bruce C. Hafen and Marie K. Hafen, *The Contrite Spirit: How the Temple Helps Us Apply Christ's Atonement* (Salt Lake City: Deseret Book, 2015).

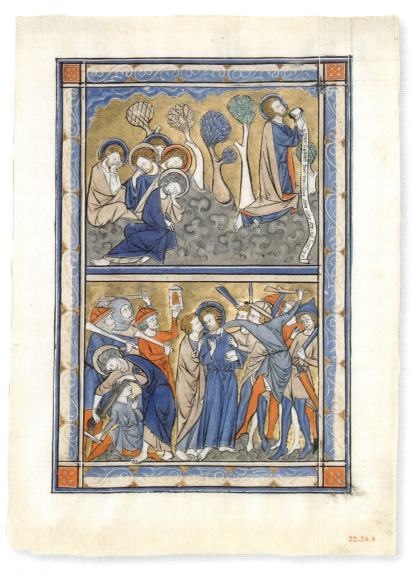

"And being in an agony he prayed more earnestly: and his sweat was as it were great drops of blood falling down to the ground" (Luke 22:44). Manuscript Leaf with the Agony in the Garden and Betrayal of Christ, from a Royal Psalter, ca. 1270. The Metropolitan Museum of Art, New York, Rogers Fund, 1922.

CHAPTER 11

THE WINEPRESS

I was in elementary school when the Washington D.C. Temple was built. It was the first temple east of the Mississippi River and is prominently situated on a hilltop along the Beltway, the major thoroughfare encircling Washington, D.C., and Arlington, Virginia: my home. I don't remember my exact age, but I clearly remember one Saturday morning when my parents explained that they were going to the temple open house and that I could join them. In a moment that I continue to regret, I told them that I didn't want to miss my favorite Saturday-morning cartoon shows. I wasn't interested in their invitation. They didn't force me, and I didn't go.

Sometimes there is a flip side to the invitations that we are offered. If we don't choose to receive the gift that we are being given, then the gift itself can stand in condemnation of our choice. Speaking of the last resurrection, Christ says that those who never chose to know him will come and stand before him. "And then shall they know that I am the Lord their God, that I am their Redeemer; but they would not be redeemed"

(Mosiah 26:26)—"would not" meaning "did not want to." These will be the people who had the opportunity to come to know Christ and receive his redeeming power but who did not want to be redeemed. The consequences of agency can be sobering and sound harsh, but remembering that we receive what we are willing to receive helps us realize that Christ is always seeking our redemption (see Doctrine and Covenants 88:32–33). He is always offering us mercy. His arms of mercy are extended to us. But his justice—his righteousness—is shown in letting us have the final word on what we want.

Keeping this perspective can help us understand the imagery of Christ and the winepress. In Isaiah 63 we see both the loving and the more sobering aspects of this image. In this prophecy, Christ is asked, "Wherefore art thou red in thine apparel, and thy garments like him that treadeth in the winefat?" (63:2). From modern-day scripture, we know that when he comes again "the Lord shall be red in his apparel, and his garments like him that treadeth in the wine-vat" (Doctrine and Covenants 133:48). In Isaiah we read that, when asked about his red garments, he shall say: "I have trodden the winepress alone; and of the people there was none with me: for I will tread them in mine anger, and trample them in my fury; and their blood shall be sprinkled upon my garments, and I will stain all my raiment" (Isaiah 63:3). The language here of the Lord's anger and fury can be hard to reconcile with the gospel message of his redeeming love. His Second Coming is also associated with judgment, and I think that we can see his role as judge and our personal accountability to him in better perspective as we dive more deeply into the imagery of Christ treading the winepress alone.

The idea of Christ as the mystical winepress was an image that was beloved in the later Middle Ages. As Christians tried to think about what the Lord's Atonement meant and how they could receive it in their lives, they knew that the sacrament, what they knew as the Eucharist, was essential. The Eucharist, the body and blood of Christ, was sacred, and they experienced partaking of it, or even seeing it, as a very holy occasion. Indeed, as time went on it became common for only priests to drink the wine, and ordinary Christians began to partake of the bread (the host) less frequently because it was seen as so holy that they feared not being worthy. At the very same time, the holiness and power in these substances was the source of widespread meditation and reverence. People tried to understand how Christ could make himself present in these substances, and they developed artistic metaphors to depict Christ as the mystic mill and the mystical winepress to show that from his body came the substances that could give spiritual life.

The imagery of Christ treading the winepress, as we have seen, has a clear foundation in the imagery of Isaiah, and this biblical image can be helpful to think through what these medieval images might be pointing us to. Physical symbols can give us a glimpse of spiritual reality. Indeed, the very physical reality of the pressing of olives seems to have stood behind the significance of Christ's suffering in a place called Gethsemane, which literally means "oil press." When olives are first pressed for oil, the initial pressing has a reddish color, reminiscent of Christ's bleeding from every pore in the garden.

Encouraging us to reflect on this symbolism whenever we see olive oil used for a blessing, President Russell M. Nelson remarked over thirty years ago: "Remember what it meant to all who had ever lived and who ever would yet live. Remember the redemptive power of healing, soothing, and ministering to those in need. Remember, just as the body of the olive, which was pressed for the oil that gave light, so the Savior was pressed. From every pore oozed the life blood of our Redeemer. And when sore trials come upon you, remember Gethsemane."[1] By slowing down to see the physical substance of olive oil as a symbol for the atoning blood of Christ, we can begin to see the spiritual truth of Christ's suffering and death as the source of healing and life.

The Lord has always used images and parables to connect physical reality with spiritual reality. Just as the pressing of olives points to the pressing of Christ, so Isaiah used the pressing of grapes to help us understand Christ's suffering. Following this metaphor, in late medieval devotional images of Christ, we can see him standing in a vat of grapes,

The image of Christ being pressed in a winepress showed his sufferings as the source of the life and mercy that we need. Theodosia-altaar, detail, 1545. Museum Catharijneconvent, Utrecht.

stomping them to produce wine, but at the same time Christ himself is being pressed and is bleeding. Sometimes it is the cross alone that presses on him and sometimes a press is depicted above his head pressing on the cross that presses on him. Often depicted as a press that turned on a screw, like a very old-fashioned printing press, these images portrayed Christ being pressed down in his suffering and his blood merging with the wine produced as he trod the winepress. Even in some depictions of Christ as a child on his mother's lap, he or Mary is portrayed holding a bunch of grapes, pointing ahead to his atoning sacrifice.

In our days, we use water in the sacrament rather than wine, and so the visual parallels of wine and Christ's blood take more imagination than in earlier Christian days. Fortunately, the sacrament hymns can help focus our meditation. Again, "Reverently and Meekly Now" encourages us to see beyond the bread and water to the spiritual truths presented with the physical realities.

> In this bread now blest for thee,
> Emblem of my body see;
> In this water or this wine,
> Emblem of my blood divine.
> Oh, remember what was done
> That the sinner might be won.
> On the cross of Calvary
> I have suffered death for thee.[2]

Looking for and seeing the redeeming sacrifice of Christ in physical symbols may take effort, but our effort allows us to behold and feel the love manifest in his gift.

We can see how early the imagery of wine as blood appears by examining the Gospel of John's description of the Savior's first miracle. In this account of Christ turning water to wine at Cana, the water becoming wine provides an important religious contrast. The water that Christ turned into wine was not just any water but was water used for ritual purification following an understanding of the law of Moses. Christ used the water found in "six waterpots of stone, after the manner of the purifying of the Jews" (John 2:6). So the external purification mandated by the law of Moses stands in contrast to the foreshadowed inner purification offered by Christ's atoning blood, symbolized by the wine.

Christ's first miracle points to and foreshadows the purpose of his mission of redemption. Through his suffering and death, he came to provide a means of holiness and sanctification that will replace the external holiness made available "after the manner of the purifying of the Jews." Through his atoning blood, we can have our garments made white; we can become clean. But to see this dimension of what the miracle teaches, we must connect the images of wine and blood in our own minds, as the

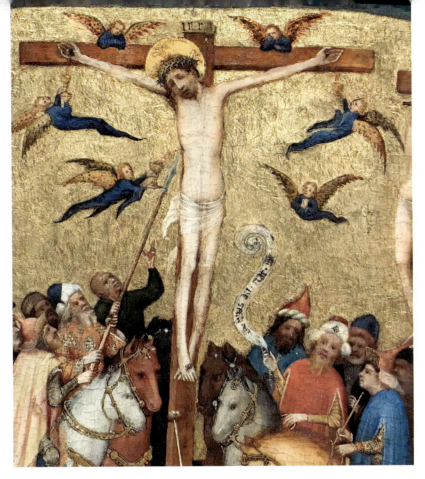

Angels were often shown collecting the blood of Christ that would nourish the faithful. Meister der hl. Veronika, The Small Calvary, detail, around 1400. Wallraf-Richartz-Museum, Köln.

early Christians—the first readers of the Gospel of John—would have done.

In the later Middle Ages, making the connection between wine and blood was not difficult. Often the images of Christ as the mystic winepress show individuals, either angels or clergymen, holding up the sacramental chalice or cup filled with the wine that was the final result of the "processing" of this mystic winepress. Similarly, many depictions of Christ on the cross also show one or more angels hovering in the air, holding a chalice to gather the blood from Christ's hands or side. There was no question for medieval believers that Christ bled to provide the blood that would nourish the faithful.

Another beloved medieval image that reinforced this metaphor of Christ's blood giving life to the faithful was the legend of the pelican. There were medieval books known as bestiaries that had fanciful descriptions of legendary animals. The pelican was one of these animals. I learned about this legend when I sang in the BYU Women's Chorus before my mission. The composer, Randall Thompson, had set an entry of one of these bestiaries to music in a beautiful song, "The Pelican," with English text by the poet Richard Wilbur. It wasn't just the stirring musical setting or the evocative language of the translation that moved me. In this song, I came to see and feel another dimension of the love of God.

The legend tells how the pelican brought its young back to life by striking its own breast with its beak. Sint-Niklaaskerk, embroidery on processional canopy. Veurne, Belgium.

In the legend the pelican takes care of its offspring, but in return they attack their parent and die as a result. The pelican then strikes its own breast with its beak and with the blood that flows out brings the children back to life. Throughout the Middle Ages, the power of self-sacrifice in the image or symbol of the pelican was repeatedly drawn or sculpted to point to Christ. This metaphor of Christ giving his own life to give new life to his offspring, the believers, joined the symbol of the mystic winepress as an extremely widespread and beloved image of Christ's redeeming blood.

Judgment and the Winepress

Both Isaiah and the book of Revelation connect the winepress with the wrath of God. We sometimes see that wrath pointed against us, but let's look more closely at the language in Revelation 19. Here we see Christ coming to rule and reign. He is "clothed with a vesture dipped in blood: and his name is called The Word of God" (19:13). Verse 15 points to his right to judge and rule: "and out of his mouth goeth a sharp sword, that with it he should smite the nations: and he shall rule them with a rod of iron." But it also stresses that "he treadeth the winepress of the fierceness and wrath of Almighty God."

Recognizing that the winepress was "the fierceness and wrath of Almighty God" is a critical point that we sometimes overlook. The consequences of our sins result in what scripture describes as the "wrath of God." To use another image, this winepress is the bitter cup that should have been ours, but Christ drank it for us. At the temple at Bountiful, directly after announcing himself as Jesus Christ, "the light and the life of the world," Christ tells the people: "I have drunk out of that bitter cup which the Father hath given me, and have glorified the Father in taking upon me the sins of the world, in the which I have suffered the will of the Father in all things from the beginning" (3 Nephi 11:11). Drinking this cup of wrath for us, "treading the winepress alone," this is what he is offering to take from us. His willingness to tread the winepress, to drink the bitter cup, also shapes the meaning of the cup that he gives us to drink.

Christ takes the cup of wrath, the cup of indignation. By drinking the bitter cup of the consequences of all that we have done to offend God, Christ frees us from what should have been our fate. He partakes of the consequences of our life and offers us instead the chance to partake of his life, to enjoy his unity with the Father and the fullness of his Spirit. The bitterness of all that we have chosen did not just disappear. He drank that bitter cup in our place. What Christ has done in treading the winepress as he suffered for our sins puts us in a relationship with him that we cannot ignore.

And so, as we read the passages about Christ treading the winepress alone, hopefully we can see the price that he paid in treading "the winepress of the fierceness and wrath of Almighty God" (Revelation 19:15). He doesn't just want us to feel sorry for him. He wants us to know that his love is so deep that, like the legend of the pelican, he shed his blood to give us life. He wants us to know that his love is so deep that he would do anything to keep us from receiving the eternal consequences of our choices. "Thus saith thy Lord the Lord, and thy God that pleadeth the cause of his people, Behold, I have taken out of thine hand the cup of trembling, even the dregs of the cup of my fury; thou shalt no more drink it again" (Isaiah 51:22). As he treads the winepress alone, he is pleading with us to accept his suffering on our behalf. That is what he wants for us more than anything else. He wants us to "no more drink" the cup of trembling and the cup of God's wrath.

How could he more fully communicate his desire to redeem us? "I have trodden the winepress alone; and of the people there was none with me" (Isaiah 63:3). None could be with him because he did this for all of us. As Abinadi testified, "Thus all mankind were lost; and behold, they would have been endlessly lost were it not that God redeemed his people from their lost and fallen state" (Mosiah 16:4). The redemption price was paid, and Christ will return in a red robe so that we will know what he suffered on our behalf in that winepress. But, as a prophet of God,

Abinadi also testified that even the redemption of Christ cannot overpower human agency (see Mosiah 16:5). He has trodden "the winepress of the fierceness and wrath of Almighty God," but we must let him take out of our hand the cup of trembling. We must let go of the cup of wrath and accept instead the blood of the covenant.

If we do not choose faith, repentance, and making and keeping covenants, we are instead choosing to persist in our "own carnal nature, and [go] on in the ways of sin and rebellion against God." Of those who make this choice, Abinadi warns that they "[remain] in [their] fallen state and the devil hath all power over [them]. Therefore [they are] as though there was no redemption made, being an enemy to God; and also is the devil an enemy to God" (Mosiah 16:5). Perhaps this is why judgment imagery is interwoven with the imagery of Christ treading the winepress alone. How we respond to his suffering on our behalf becomes our judgment. Without choosing to receive his gift with our faith and repentance, coming unto him on the covenant path, we will someday know that he redeemed us, but we did not want to be redeemed. He offers to take away the cup of wrath and replace it with the cup of his blood, his life, his fullness. We decide. We will receive what we are willing to receive.

NOTES

1. Russell M. Nelson, "Why This Holy Land?," *Ensign*, December 1989, 13.
2. Joseph L. Townsend, "Reverently and Meekly Now," in *Hymns* (Salt Lake City: The Church of Jesus Christ of Latter-day Saints, 1985), no. 185.

CHAPTER 12

PIETÀ

Most of us remember attending a fast and testimony sacrament meeting when we were young or first introduced to the Church. We see people getting up to the pulpit to share their testimony and think, "Why are people crying?" I am sure I asked my parents that when I was little. After many years of watching people bear testimony, as a teenager I went up to share things that I had really come to know. I don't remember what I said, but I remember how I felt. I felt a powerful witness of the reality of what I was saying, and even when I finished and went to sit with my family on our bench, I was almost doubled over with tears. The image that came to mind, maybe from a song or a Bible verse, was being held in the bosom of Abraham. I was enveloped with a feeling of God's love. And I remember hearing a sibling ask my parents why I was crying.

Tears are interesting. We can cry from sorrow. We can cry from joy. We can cry when we are scared or despondent. We can cry when we are overcome with relief and gratitude. Sometimes tears can be an automatic emotional response. We talk of certain kinds of movies as "tearjerkers." They tap into deep emotional responses. So, with the range and complexity of things that can bring us to tears, I can't develop some equation between our love for the Savior and a response of crying. There is a difference between sentimentality and spirituality. There is a difference between having a heart-warming experience and receiving a spiritual witness. At the same time, some deep spiritual experiences can, on special occasions, bring people to tears.

How Do We Respond?

The opposite of feeling a spiritual response is described in the Book of Mormon as hardening our hearts. Some people harden their hearts until they are "past feeling" (1 Nephi 17:45; Moroni 9:20). Crying in response to the manifestation of the love of God may not equate with spiritual health, but *not* feeling anything may be a symptom of spiritual sickness. If God's mercy and love leave us cold, then that can be a warning that our heart has started to harden and we must make changes to retain our change of heart.[1]

Christ explained this danger to the Pharisee named Simon. Simon was complaining about the woman who had intruded into his home to find Jesus and then "stood at his feet behind him weeping" (Luke 7:38). She was so overcome with love and gratitude that she washed Christ's feet with her tears. Christ pointed out that, in contrast, Simon's heart was so hardened that he had not even given Christ the normal courtesy due a visitor: "I entered into thine house, thou gavest me no water for my feet: but she hath washed my feet with tears, and wiped them with the hairs of her head" (Luke 7:44). Simon had been a cold and distant host, withholding hospitality, keeping himself removed from Christ. The woman's emotional response, on the other hand, was extravagant and overwhelming. Christ's diagnosis of Simon's spiritual health was that he had not felt the love of forgiveness. "Her sins, which are many, are forgiven; for she loved much: but to whom little is forgiven, the same loveth little" (7:47).

We don't know the backstory of that woman or her relationship with the Savior, but her tears and her actions of worship manifest a love born of deep gratitude. She had experienced redemption through Christ. The burden of her guilt had been removed. Simon, a Pharisee trying very hard to live a holy life, looked at this woman, "a sinner" (Luke 7:39), and could easily believe that *she* needed forgiveness. His problem was that he could not believe that *he* needed forgiveness. So, as we see in this account, it is not the presence of Christ that brings love and gratitude so great that we would kneel to wash his feet with our tears. They were both with him, but each had a very different response to him. Only feeling the love and forgiveness of Christ can produce the love and gratitude that may produce those tears.

Learning to Respond

In the later Middle Ages, devotional art and devotional texts consciously sought to model an appropriate response to Christ. There was a strong sense of how critical a response to him was for human salvation. There was a technical term for the response that devout late medieval Christians were taught to cultivate: *compassio*, or "compassion." Christ's suffering was his passion, and so the viewer or reader was encouraged to respond by suffering *with* him, *com-passio*. His suffering was an expression of his love for humanity, and in return humans needed to express their love for him.

To cultivate this response of "compassion," individuals were encouraged to feel as though they were present with Christ during his suffering and death. Not only were they to imagine themselves into the scenes of the passion, but they were also encouraged to seek to suffer with him through this imaginative participation. In the *Meditationes vitae Christi*, a very influential devotional text, a description of Christ's suffering is woven together with a direct appeal to behold the sufferings. The listener or reader is taught how to feel compassion through repetitive language that echoes the Lord's experience. "The Lord is therefore stripped and bound to a column and scourged in various ways.... Again and again, repeatedly, closer and closer, it is done, bruise upon bruise, and cut upon cut, until not only the torturers but also the spectators are tired." The vivid narrative emphasizes the repetition of the blows. The text then explains the effect that pondering this account should have: "Here, then, *consider Him diligently* for a long time; and *if you do not feel compassion at this point*, you may count yours as a heart of stone."[2] The account seeks to make Christ's suffering present and moving to the audience.

The *Meditationes vitae Christi* continues to give clear directions on how to respond as the narrative continues: "Look at Him well, then, as He goes along bowed down by the cross and gasping aloud. Feel as much compassion for Him as you can, placed in such anguish, in renewed derision."[3] By emphasizing the audience's role to "look" and "feel," this devotional text explains how to have personal involvement with Christ's carrying of the cross through imaginative and emotional participation.

Medieval theologians taught that sharing his suffering was the means by which the blessings of Christ's suffering were received. This started back in the era of monastic meditation on the suffering of Christ, laying the foundation for the Franciscans in the thirteenth century. Participation in Christ's suffering became imperative in twelfth-century Cistercian piety because their theologians understood it as the means by which one can experience God's love. Bernard of Clairvaux expresses this connection by exhorting the listeners: "Let us learn his humility, imitate his gentleness, *embrace his love, share his sufferings*, be washed in his blood."[4]

Participation in Christ's suffering not only allows an individual to feel Christ's love, but also opens up the path to eternal glory. Passages such as Paul's comment to the Corinthians give us a way to make meaning out of the sufferings that we go through in mortality: "As ye are partakers of the sufferings, so shall ye be also of the consolation" (2 Corinthians 1:7). Speaking for Christ, Bernard explains that "he who meditates on my death and, following my example, mortifies his members which belong to this earth, has eternal life; meaning, if you share in my sufferings, you will partake of my glory."⁵ Likewise, Peter explained, "inasmuch as ye are partakers of Christ's sufferings; that, when his glory shall be revealed, ye may be glad also with exceeding joy" (1 Peter 4:13).

The Cistercians' emphasis on the suffering of Christ and the individual's response to that suffering was a major shift in medieval theology and spirituality. When we understand this theological model, we can have a better appreciation for the dimensions of late medieval piety that included taking active steps to experience suffering, in imitation of Christ, by making their own bodies to suffer. Understanding their beliefs helps make it clearer why people would voluntarily seek out suffering as a way to feel closer to the Savior and receive his mercy.

One of the blessings of the Restoration is a clearer sense of "how to come unto him and be saved" (1 Nephi 15:14). Through the teachings of the Book of Mormon and the restoration of priesthood authority and ordinances, the doctrine of Christ is taught and enacted. So, while we can understand and appreciate the devotion of late medieval Christians, we do not need to join them in seeking out suffering with Christ. I have taken comfort through the years in Elder Neal A. Maxwell's words affirming that we need not volunteer for suffering.

> There are many who suffer so much more than the rest of us: some go agonizingly; some go quickly; some are healed; some are given more time; some seem to linger. There are variations in our trials but no immunities. Thus, the scriptures cite the fiery furnace and fiery trials (see Dan. 3:6–26; 1 Pet. 4:12). Those who emerge successfully from their varied and fiery furnaces have experienced the grace of the Lord, which He says is sufficient (see Ether 12:27). Even so, brothers and sisters, such emerging individuals do not rush to line up in front of another fiery furnace in order to get an extra turn!⁶

One of the greatest clarifications of the Restoration is not only the affirmation that Christ has suffered for us, but also the additional witness that he has truly suffered *with* us in all things (see Alma 7:11–13).

Even though we don't need to seek out suffering with Christ, the late medieval practice of seeking to make Christ's suffering real for us can be a benefit to us. Seeking to put ourselves into the stories of these events can be a valuable mental exercise. This is much like the practice of likening that Nephi encourages (see 1 Nephi 19:23). In emphasizing our response to Christ's suffering, we don't want to be emotionally manipulated or to manipulate others with this exercise, but we do want to learn from others and learn of Christ. Seeing how others have been changed by the love of God can help us come to understand the reality of these experiences. Seeing the impact that Christ had on them can allow us to consider our response to him.

As we try to keep Christ's atoning sacrifice alive for us, we can read scriptural accounts closely and take the responses of the participants as models of how to respond to Christ. Studying these texts with an eye to others' response to Christ can be like listening to the testimonies of others. Their responses to Christ can help us learn how to respond to our own experiences with Christ and his Spirit. Seeing others respond with love and gratitude can help us learn what having a softened heart can look like. Seeing them turn away and harden their hearts can be a warning.

Modeling Response

In late medieval devotional art, presenting models of response was a central aim. Mary was the ideal of compassion and the principal model of response. Perhaps the most widespread way Mary's compassion was portrayed was in her sorrow at the cross. There was an entire genre of hymns recounting how she felt to see her son on the cross and inviting the listener to feel with her, the most famous of which is "Stabat Mater dolorosa." Some visual artists, most strikingly Rogier van der Weyden, portray her swooning at the cross in a pose echoing Christ's curved body being taken down from the cross. In addition to this image of Mary at the cross, there were many other scenes, known as the Seven Sorrows of Mary, that depict her response of compassion.

In the New Testament, we learn that when Mary took the infant Christ to the temple, she met a man who recognized the baby Jesus as the Messiah. Simeon's prophecy was not only about Jesus's role as the Messiah but also about Mary's future as his mother. She was told that "a sword shall pierce through thy own soul also" (Luke 2:35). This prophecy was visually depicted with images of Mary with a sword pointed at her heart, or, in some depictions, seven swords. The tradition of the Seven Sorrows of Mary is drawn from seven mostly biblical scenes when Mary was a witness of the suffering of her son. These seven sorrows became a focus of devotional meditation that is still practiced and include Simeon's prophecy, the flight into Egypt, losing Christ at the temple, meeting Christ on his way to Calvary, seeing Christ on the cross, the descent from the cross, and the burial.

The most famous image of Mary's sorrow, the Pietà, is not described in the scriptural narrative, but stands as a moment of devotional reflection between Christ's descent from the cross and his burial. It is a private moment. Depictions of the descent and the lamentation portray many people looking at Christ's body, but in the Pietà, the dead Christ is held by his mother on her lap. Our focus is on her response to him. The term *pietà* is Italian for compassion or mercy. The most famous Pietà, of course, is Michelangelo's *Pietà*, which stands in St. Peter's Basilica in Rome. It is made of white Carrara marble and depicts the solemn and beautiful sadness and submission of Mary as she feels compassion for Christ; we can feel compassion for her and through that increase our compassion for Christ. We see her loss as she cradles her dead son and presents him to us for our meditation and reflection.

Before this portrayal of sorrow in the perfection of human form and beauty by this master of the Italian Renaissance, earlier versions of the Pietà were widespread in Northern Europe. These depictions were usually carved in wood and painted, although some were also of alabaster and limestone. They provided a less elegant but even more evocative and emotional portrayal of both the dead Christ and Mary's grief. Part of the

FINDING CHRIST IN THE COVENANT PATH

elegance of Michelangelo's *Pietà* comes from the body of Christ being proportionately smaller than Mary so he can be easily held on her lap.

In the Northern wooden images Christ's body is often large and awkward. We see Mary straining to hold him as his body and head slump back. Her face looks on him and reflects her grief and sorrow. Rather than being a pure white marble, these wooden images were painted vivid colors. Christ's wounds are often carved deep and sometimes the drops of blood are not only painted red, but also carved to an exaggerated size. Sometimes Mary's tears are also carved and elevated, dripping down her face. The immediacy of his death as well as her grief is present for those who meditate on this image.

In addition to the depictions of the devotional scene of the Pietà, another invitation to imitate the response of Mary can be found in a focus on Mary's and others' tears, often in scenes known in art literature as the Crucifixion, Deposition (or descent from the cross), and Lamentation. Especially famous for his de-

The image of the Pietà models a response of love and grief in response to Christ's death. Unnaer Pietà, about 1380. LWL-Museum für Kunst und Kultur, Münster.

piction of tears is Rogier van der Weyden. His depictions of sorrow can move the viewer to grief and prompt reflection on his or her own feelings

The tears shown in many devotional paintings modeled responses of sorrow, love, and gratitude for Christ's death on our behalf. Rogier van der Weyden, The Entombment of Christ, *detail, ca. 1460–64 (taken in Maritshuis, The Hague). Galleria degli Uffizi, Florence.*

about the suffering and death of Christ. How real is this for me? How much does this matter to me? Is his suffering and death present to me?

Models of Love, Models of Response

Learning who Christ is and what he has done for us is the study of a lifetime. We can learn from doctrinal discussions, but getting information is not the same thing as lived experience and personal witness. Coming to know Christ can sometimes be triangulated through knowing the love of someone else who is a witness of his love. That might be part of why the image of the Pietà is so powerful. We know doctrinally that God so loved the world that he gave his only begotten Son, but in the Pietà we can see the love of a mother who also gave her son. Seeing a mother holding her dead child can speak to deep human emotions of grief and loss.

As we seek to feel the love of God manifest in the suffering and death of Christ, sometimes the love and sacrifice of a mother can give us a framework and a model to feel and respond to God's love. The maternal images Christ connects with himself are not coincidental. For most of us, the foundational love that grounds our lives is the love of our mother.

Christ compares his open arms to the wings of a mother hen ready to protect her offspring: "O ye house of Israel whom I have spared, how oft will I gather you as a hen gathereth her chickens under her wings, if ye will repent and return unto me with full purpose of heart" (3 Nephi 10:6). He asks, "Can a woman forget her sucking child, that she should not have compassion on the son of her womb? yea, they may forget, yet will I not forget thee. Behold, I have graven thee upon the palms of my hands" (Isaiah 49:15–16).

We know the gathering and protective love of a mother, and reflecting on that love can point us to the divine love that may transcend our understanding. His scarred hands bear witness to his love, but sometimes we can feel that love indirectly through other people.

I don't know that we need to take up the devotional image of the Pietà to appreciate the love of God, but Mary's response is a powerful

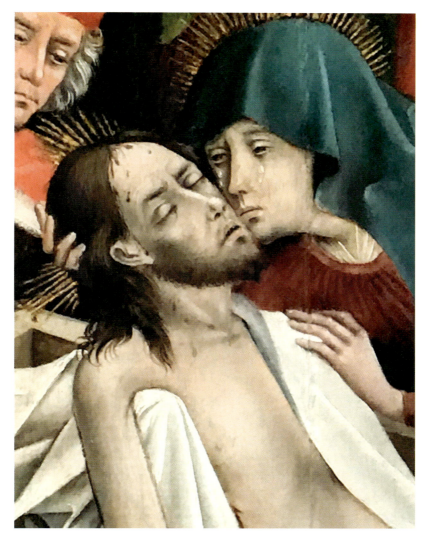

The image of Mary's love and grief helps us increase our love for Christ. Johann Koerbecke, Six Panels from Marienfeld, *detail, about 1443/57. LWL-Museum für Kunst und Kultur, Münster.*

model for us in our efforts to worship. I find it fascinating that in 1 Nephi 11 when Nephi sought to know the meaning of the tree of life, the first thing he is shown is the Virgin Mary alone and then again holding the Christ child.

Only when Nephi sees Mary and her child Jesus does the angel say unto him: "Behold the Lamb of God, yea, even the Son of the Eternal Father! Knowest thou the meaning of the tree which thy father saw?" (1 Nephi 11:21). It was at that point that Nephi could respond: "Yea, it is the love of God, which sheddeth itself abroad in the hearts of the children of men; wherefore, it is the most desirable above all things" (11:22).

Mary's willingness to be the mother of the Son of God and then to watch him die as the Lamb of God gives us a model to reflect on and to emulate: "Behold the handmaid [servant] of the Lord; be it unto me according to thy word" (Luke 1:38). Her love as a mother can point us to Christ. Through her role and her example, we can receive a revelation of the love of God.

Textual Models of Response

One fall semester at Brigham Young University, the year before I served a mission, I remember sitting on a little grassy hill on campus, talking with some friends. It was a sunny, pleasant afternoon and we were relaxed, talking about the semester, life, and the future. As our conversation wound along, I mentioned how I wanted to more fully understand Christ's Atonement and what it meant for me. Within the next couple of weeks President Benson gave powerful talks in general conference that worked on me and motivated me to start studying the Book of Mormon daily. As they do for most people, the early stories in the Book of Mormon came alive to me with the accounts of Nephi's faith and diligence. I started to see how he responded to the Lord and to the promptings of the Spirit. What I was reading helped me think about my own life and helped me learn to respond to promptings that I was starting to recognize. Nephi's model of response was invaluable for my spiritual growth.

Textual models of response may be one of the great gifts we have in scriptures. In addition to doctrine and teachings, we see how people change as they come to know and understand Christ and his atoning sacrifice. This is particularly true in the Book of Mormon. It truly serves as another testament of Jesus Christ from the first to the last chapters by showing us how individuals responded to Christ. In a way similar to reflecting on devotional art, in the text of the Book of Mormon other people's feelings can help us learn how to feel. Other people's examples can help us learn how to act.

The Book of Mormon is in many ways a manual of how to respond to Christ, with both positive and negative models. We can see this from the very beginning in the lives of Lehi and Nephi and the choices they make to respond to what they come to know. Lehi "fear[ed] exceedingly" for Laman and Lemuel when he saw they would not come to the tree (1 Nephi 8:4). Nephi was "grieved because of the hardness of their hearts" and he "cried unto the Lord for them" (1 Nephi 2:18).

The people of King Benjamin "[view] themselves in their own carnal state" (Mosiah 4:2), cry out for mercy through Christ's atoning blood, and then witness that because of the influence of the Spirit they "have no more disposition to do evil, but to do good continually" (Mosiah 5:2). We see an example of how to respond to Christ in the examples of the converted Lamanites who are "overpowered with joy" (Alma 19:14) and are so determined to break from their past that they bury their weapons deep in the earth and swear not to fight again.

Some of the most compelling examples of responding to Christ and the message of his Atonement are found in the accounts of Alma the Younger and the sons of Mosiah. We can see how they lived before they came to know Christ and how feeling the love and mercy of Christ changed their hearts. We see them knowing of Christ but rejecting him and teaching others to reject him. Then later we are able to see the results of them turning to Christ in faith, asking for mercy. As Alma remembered his father's teaching "concerning the coming of one Jesus Christ, a Son of God, to atone for the sins of the world" (Alma 36:17), he cried within his heart, "O Jesus, thou Son of God, have mercy on me, who am in the gall of bitterness, and am encircled about by the everlasting chains of death" (36:18). As we seek to learn for ourselves what mercy is and how to receive it, this plea can help us learn the only way to find redemption.

Much of the Book of Mormon is composed of the extensive accounts of the life and service of Alma the Younger and the sons of Mosiah. We see their response of faith in a time of crisis. We are able to watch the change in their lives, their complete conversion, how they lived the rest of their lives to bring others to know the joy of redemption.

Because of their faith in Christ and the repentance it brought, we can see that it is possible to have one's feelings and motivations dramatically changed: "they could not bear that any human soul should perish; yea, even the very thoughts that any soul should endure endless torment did cause them to quake and tremble" (Mosiah 28:3). These examples of response to Christ's atoning sacrifice model a life of discipleship and conversion for us. Just as those seeking to learn how to respond to Christ had models in late medieval devotional imagery and texts, we have been blessed with a volume of scripture that shows us "how to come unto him and be saved" (1 Nephi 15:14).

Having a change of heart is one of the primary themes of the Book of Mormon, and it pushes us to watch ourselves to see our response to Christ. Are we becoming hardened, coarsened to things of the Spirit? Are we becoming less grateful? Are we feeling more entitled? Are we feeling casual about the things of God? Viewing and considering responses to Christ can help us consider our own response. We can deepen our ability to respond by pondering and emulating responses of gratitude, love, and awe at his sacrificial death. As our love and gratitude deepen, we move from responses of feeling love to living out the love we feel.

Notes

1. Dale G. Renlund, "Preserving the Heart's Mighty Change," *Ensign*, November 2009, 97–99.

2. *Meditationes vitae Christi: Meditations on the Life of Christ; An Illustrated Manuscript of the Fourteenth Century*, trans. Isa Ragusa, ed. Isa Ragusa and Rosalie B.

Green, Princeton Monographs in Art and Archeology XXXV (Princeton: Princeton University Press, 1961), 328–29.

3. *Meditationes vitae Christi*, 331.

4. Bernard, "In Praise of the Virgin Mother," homily 3:14, in *Magnificat: Homilies in Praise of the Blessed Virgin Mary*, trans. Marie-Bernard Saïd and Grace Perigo, Cistercian Fathers Series 18 (Kalamazoo, MI: Cistercian Publications, 1979), 44; emphasis added.

5. Bernard, *De diligendo Deo*, chapter IV: 11; *On Loving God*, trans. Emero Stiegman, Cistercian Fathers Series 13 B (Kalamazoo, MI: Cistercian Publications, 1973), 13.

6. Neal A. Maxwell, "From Whom All Blessings Flow," *Ensign*, May 1997, 11–12.

Our "redemption [is] . . . brought to pass through the power, and sufferings, and death of Christ, and his resurrection and ascension into heaven" (Mosiah 18:2). Jean Pucelle, The Hours of Jeanne d'Evreux, Queen of France, fol. 82v, detail, ca. 1324–28. The Metropolitan Museum of Art, New York, The Cloisters Collection, 1954.

CHAPTER 13

MAN OF SORROWS

As humans, we have an interesting blind spot. Sometimes in defending the truth of one thing, we forget another element needed to make up the whole picture of what is real. We are focused, but sometimes our desire to focus closes our eyes to other dimensions of reality. I had an interesting conversation during my first year in college that illustrates this problem. I was a first-year student at Wellesley College, a women's college in the Boston area. There were just four of us Latter-day Saints, all in that incoming class. We attended church together in Cambridge and had a small institute meeting on campus weekly.

Occasionally we ate together. I remember one meal very vividly. At this dinner, probably by appointment, the four of us met in a dining hall with two or three evangelical students. We sat at a round wooden table in high-backed wooden chairs and talked about doctrine while we ate. One topic we discussed was our different understandings of what it meant to be the children of God. The gist of the conversation, as I remember it, was *their* insistence that we become the children of God by being born again and *our* insistence that everyone is a child of God already.

As Latter-day Saints, we were excited about what we knew about the premortal world and our relationship with Heavenly Father. We were grateful for spiritual truths that our fellow students didn't have without the Restoration. What we didn't appreciate at the time was that what they were arguing for was true as well. It wasn't an either/or situation but a both/and.

We are beloved spirit sons and daughters of Heavenly Parents, but we also need to become the children of God by being born again. In our discussion, we Latter-day Saints latched on to what made us different and hadn't really explored the gospel truth of their witness. Not only the Bible but also the Book of Mormon confirms our need to be born again, to take the name of Christ upon us and become his spiritual children through covenant. Having more doesn't mean that we should dismiss what we might not understand yet. It took me additional years and deeper study of the Book of Mormon to learn for myself what those evangelical students were testifying of that evening.

As members of The Church of Jesus Christ of Latter-day Saints, we sometimes pride ourselves in not using crosses or crucifixes in our church buildings. We emphasize our focus on the resurrected Christ. We are grateful for the witness of prophets and apostles in "The Living Christ" and know that he will again return to rule and reign.[1]

In the first chapter of the book of Revelation we read of Christ's appearance to John: "Fear not; I am the first and the last: I am he that liveth, and was dead; and, behold, I am alive for evermore" (Revelation 1:17–18). Christ is alive forevermore. He lives. But it is not insignificant that he also testifies that he was dead. Maintaining our vision of the Risen Christ while keeping an awareness of his atoning, sacrificial death is critical to having a full understanding of his nature.

In medieval devotional imagery, an extraordinary image developed that allowed people to view both the living and the sacrificed Christ simultaneously. This image is known as the Man of Sorrows, or *Imago pietatis*. It started as an image of Christ bearing the wounds of his crucifixion, but upright, not laying down as a dead body would do. It was not

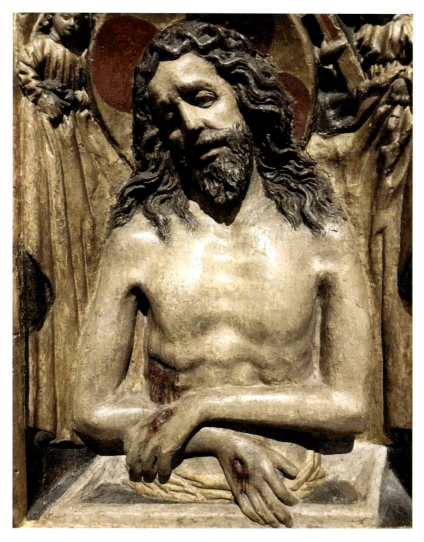

The image of the Man of Sorrows, or Imago pietatis, *allowed people to view both the living and the sacrificed Christ simultaneously. Diptych depicting Our Lady of Sorrows and the Man of Sorrows framed by boxes for relics, detail, second half of the fifteenth century. Museum Schnütgen, Köln.*

part of the visual narrative sequence of the descent from the cross, the lamentation over his body, or burial. This image was a devotional image that focused on a depiction or portrait of Christ.

Showing Christ's head, arms, and torso standing upright in a tomb, this portrait pointed to the Resurrection. Initially, however, the depiction was muted as his head tilted to the left side with his eyes closed, as in death. This image was borrowed in Western Europe from an Eastern Orthodox icon, but over time, it changed in its new home. Little by little, depictions in the West started to show the hands of Christ not just hanging down, crossed in front of him, but moving and pointing subtly to his side wound.

As the depictions of the Man of Sorrows changed to emphasize the living Christ, they started to show Christ with his eyes open. He increasingly looked at his audience and sometimes lifted his hands to show the wounds. With time, the depictions moved from being just the upper half of his body to depictions of his whole body, standing and bearing the marks of the crucifixion. These images usually emphasized not only the wounds, but also showed him continuing to bleed, emphasizing the immediacy of his suffering and death. Depictions of the Man of Sorrows also often showed him surrounded by the *Arma Christi* so that one image portrayed the entire story of his suffering, death, and resurrection.

The Man of Sorrows was not an either/or depiction. It was emphatically a both/and. Christ was shown in the tomb with his wounds, but he was not the dead Christ. He was the living Christ manifesting himself as the Lamb of God, sacrificed for the sins of the world. Through these devotional images, his death and resurrection were present and visible for all to see and ponder.

Behold the Wounds

As we think about the Lamb slain from the foundation of the world, we can also know that he is the life and the light of the world: Christ as the sacrifice and Christ as the living Word. We don't have to pick which one

MAN OF SORROWS

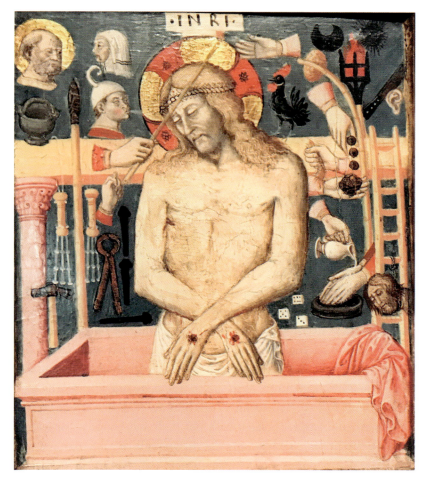

The Man of Sorrows was often accompanied by the Arma Christi so that one image portrayed the entire story of his suffering, death, and resurrection. Christ as the Man of Sorrows, with the "Arma Christi," detail, last quarter of the fifteenth century. Wallraf-Richartz-Museum, Köln.

to focus on because we can't have one without the other. He is the Lamb slain from the foundation of the world, and he is the Word of God who was with God and who was God. We cannot understand who he is and what he is offering by choosing one or the other. We can't have faith unto salvation without understanding both dimensions of his being.

In Alma 33 Alma explains the meaning of the word, which he has compared to a seed. He promises that if we plant and nurture this word with faith, diligence, patience, and long-suffering, it will grow up in us unto everlasting life. The word or message that we are to plant and nourish with our faith and diligence is "the Son of God, that he will come to redeem his people, and that *he shall suffer and die to atone for their sins; and that he shall rise again from the dead*, which shall bring to pass the resurrection, that all men shall stand before him, to be judged at the last and judgment day, according to their works" (Alma 33:22). Christ is the word. The message of his suffering, death, and resurrection is what we must focus on. As we seek to exercise our faith in the redemption that Christ offers, we must focus on both his suffering and death *and* his rising again from the dead. We can't give one or the other priority.

Christ repeatedly presents himself to us in ways that emphasize both his life and his death. The evening of Easter Sunday, he appeared in a closed room to his frightened apostles. Seeing that they were scared and that they thought they were seeing a spirit, Christ showed his wounds as a witness of his identity: "Why are ye troubled? and why do thoughts arise in your hearts? Behold my hands and my feet, that it is I myself: handle me, and see; for a spirit hath not flesh and bones, as ye see me have" (Luke 24:38–39). Not only did the wounds in his hands and feet show his identity, but they also became a source of comfort. As we behold him in his totality, we can realize that we need not be troubled or afraid. His redeeming love and his victory over death give him power, and that victory is visible through the marks in his hands and feet.

We see the exact same pattern in the Americas when Christ appeared at the temple at Bountiful. The people were afraid, and Christ's words of comfort to them focused on the message that he bore inscribed in his own body. After "stretch[ing] forth his hand," Christ testified of both his life and his death. "Behold, I am Jesus Christ, whom the prophets testified shall come into the world. And behold, I am the light and the life of the world; and I have drunk out of that bitter cup which the Father hath given me, and have glorified the Father in taking upon me the sins of the world, in the which I have suffered the will of the Father in all things from the beginning" (3 Nephi 11:9–11). Christ's identity as "the light and the life of the world" cannot be separated from his suffering and death in which he "[drank] out of that bitter cup" on our behalf.

Not only does Christ teach the gathered people of the two dimensions of his nature, as the one who lives and was slain, but he also invites them to come to know for themselves. "Arise and come forth unto me, that ye may thrust your hands into my side, and also that ye may feel the prints of the nails in my hands and in my feet, that ye may know that I am the God of Israel, and the God of the whole earth, and have been slain for the sins of the world" (3 Nephi 11:14). The invitation to a personal experience was not just seeing him, but touching his side wound and the prints of the nails. This extraordinary experience was offered to each person there.

Christ's invitation is that we come to behold and experience the simultaneous reality of his infinite life and his atoning death. We need to know for ourselves that he lives as our God and that, *as God*, he has given himself to be slain for the sins of the world. Only by embracing his infinite light and life combined with his suffering and atoning death can we have faith to repent and to follow his covenant path.

This is the invitation that he gives when he says: "Look unto me in every thought; doubt not, fear not. Behold the wounds which pierced my side, and also the prints of the nails in my hands and feet" (Doctrine and Covenants 6:36–37). What does it take to replace doubt and fear with hope and faith? Where can we look to have confidence that all of our wrongs, failures, and weaknesses will not be a permanent barrier to a peaceful and joyous future?

Many have suffered and died, but only the suffering and death of an infinite being can substitute for another's sin. As Amulek testified: "nothing which is short of an infinite atonement . . . will suffice for the sins of the world" and therefore "that great and last sacrifice will be the Son of

God, yea, infinite and eternal" (Alma 34:12, 14). Trusting in a vicarious, substitutionary sacrifice cannot mean looking to another human being to suffer for us. We need to know, as Abinadi did, that "God himself shall come down among the children of men, and shall redeem his people" (Mosiah 15:1). His wounds and nail marks are his witness to us that he has succeeded. They are his witness that, through him, we have succeeded if we trust and follow him.

Part of beholding his victorious wounds can come through reading and hearing the witnesses of those to whom it is "given to know," those who are ordained as witnesses (Doctrine and Covenants 42:65). But part of knowing comes through our own personal experiences with Christ. We can feel his Spirit testify to the truth of his suffering, death, and resurrection as we ask for mercy and feel forgiveness and his redeeming love. We are also privileged to have experiences through ordinances that allow us to not only behold but also to symbolically participate in the gift of the Atonement. The ordinances point to Christ's Atonement and help us know how to receive that power in our own life. As we will continue to explore, the ordinances connect us to Christ, and they point to a new kind of life that we can have in him. We come to know him more fully as we become more like him.

Note

1. "The Living Christ: The Testimony of the Apostles," *Ensign*, April 2000, 2.

CHAPTER 14

STIGMATA

e often think of knowledge as information in our mind, but there is an older sense of knowing that points to what we have become through our experience. When the Lord said, "This is life eternal, that they might know thee the only true God, and Jesus Christ, whom thou hast sent" (John 17:3), he wasn't promising eternal life to those who have the biggest information database about God. Knowing in this context is connected to becoming.[1]

In the spring of 2005, I learned something about knowledge and becoming. I attended a professional conference that happened to take place during the last days of Pope John Paul II's life. My return trip included a long layover in Atlanta, where I spent several hours watching the funeral on a CNN broadcast. As I watched the celebration of the funeral Mass, I reflected on the ease and naturalness with which Cardinal Ratzinger—soon to become Pope Benedict XVI—officiated. I had grown up down the street from a large Catholic high school and had attended Mass with my friends from the neighborhood, but the mammoth scale of this funeral Mass invited attention.

As I watched that airport television monitor, I reflected on the kind of knowledge that was on display in the ritual actions of the celebration of the Mass: a knowledge of what to do, how to hold oneself. This liturgical action represented a kind of embodied knowledge. This was action without thought in the sense that it was natural, embodied. It was what the individual was. In watching it, I wondered what would be involved in learning this and what it would mean to the one who embodied it.

The embodiment of knowledge I observed as an outsider caused me to reflect on knowledge and how it is conveyed in ritual and ordinance. The possibility of coming to a knowledge of God is repeated throughout the scriptures. I believe that our contemporary understanding of knowledge as acquiring a body of information is a tremendous barrier in understanding and receiving a fulfillment of those promises.

Elder Dallin H. Oaks discusses the more ancient concept of knowledge in his classic talk "The Challenge to Become." He observes that "the Apostle Paul taught that the Lord's teachings and teachers were given that we may all attain 'the measure of the stature of the fulness of Christ' (Ephesians 4:1). This process requires far more than acquiring knowledge. It is not even enough for us to be convinced of the gospel; we must act and think so that we are converted by it. In contrast to the institutions of the world, which teach us to know something, the gospel of Jesus Christ challenges us to become something."[2] I believe that knowledge as it is referred to in the language of scripture differs from that acquired in the "institutions of the world."

Knowledge in a scriptural sense is not what we know, but what we are, what we have become. Knowledge is knowing how to do things, how to be in situations. This knowledge is not abstract but embodied, and it is modeled for us in the ritual action of ordinances. The ordinances point to a way of being that we can achieve through the process of conversion; they model a way of being in which we know God.

It can be challenging for us to think of ordinances as a way of conveying knowledge. The symbols and nonverbal communication of the ordinances do not fit our contemporary model of what knowledge is. Here again, the images of the Middle Ages can bridge our modern ways of thinking with ancient concepts that the scriptures and ordinances present us with.

Embodying the Image of Christ

In the later Middle Ages, the idea of becoming like Christ was seen to be most fully exemplified in the life of St. Francis of Assisi. After a worldly youth, he experienced a conversion to Christ that led him to reject the status, riches, and power available to him through his wealthy family. Instead, he chose to follow Christ by serving in degrading conditions, caring for lepers and the poor. He lived to glorify Christ in all that he did.

As the son of a wealthy cloth merchant, Francis gave up his expensive clothes as a symbol of his rejection of worldly values, visible status, and prestige. He and his followers "were satisfied with a single tunic, often patched inside and out. Nothing about it was refined, rather it appeared lowly and rough so that in it they seemed completely crucified to the world"[3]—his biographer's reference to Galatians 6:14: "But God forbid that I should glory, save in the cross of our Lord Jesus Christ, by whom the world is crucified unto me, and I unto the world."

An example of Francis's willingness to serve and identify with the poor as a means of identifying with Christ is captured in this quotation given by his biographer, Thomas of Celano: "He used to say: 'Anyone who curses the poor insults Christ whose noble banner the poor carry, since Christ made himself poor for us in this world.'" The biographer connects that view of Christ to Francis's life of service. "That is also why, when he met poor people burdened with wood or other heavy loads, he would offer his own weak shoulders to help them."[4]

Bonaventure, a later biographer, explains Francis's emphasis on becoming poor—his practice of asceticism was not merely to deprive the

St. Francis was believed to have been changed into the image of Christ through his life of discipleship and his response of love beholding Christ's suffering. Kruisdood van Christus met stigmatisatie van Franciscus, end of the fifteenth century. Museum Catharijneconvent, Utrecht.

body, but to conform himself to the crucified Christ by crucifying the "flesh with its passions and desires."[5] Francis's poverty was an imitation of Christ because "poverty was the close companion of the Son of God"[6] and because "this is the royal dignity which the Lord Jesus assumed when he *became poor* for us that he might enrich us by *his poverty.*"[7] Poverty was participation. Francis submitted to the "mortification" of giving up his wealthy apparel in order to "carry externally in his body the cross of Christ."[8] Francis did all of this in the imitation of Christ and in memory of Christ's sacrifice, living out Christ's example of servanthood and ministering. Because of this imitation, within the Franciscan tradition Francis is described as an *alter Christus*, another Christ.

As an outward sign of the inward reality of who he had become in following the example of Christ, Francis was understood to have received the stigmata, the marks of the wounds of Christ, in his own body. The life that he lived following Christ changed him. Francis's love for Christ and his imitation of Christ's humility and service was understood to have changed him into Christ's image. Bonaventure recorded that Francis was changed into the image of Christ because beholding him "fastened to a cross pierced his soul with a sword of compassionate sorrow."[9] All that Francis did and became was a response to the love of Christ manifest in his suffering and death.

We don't need to come to any conclusion about the historical experience of Francis to appreciate the symbolic power of the stigmata. The image and idea of the stigmata are powerful to contemplate, whether or not we can know what really happened to him. Depictions of St. Francis with the stigmata were spread throughout Europe in the later Middle Ages, and his image communicated the message that the ideal of imitating Christ was possible. St. Francis was an exemplar of knowing Christ in the sense of following him and, thus, becoming like him.

The idea of knowing as becoming can be understood as embodied knowledge, being both spiritually and physically changed through following Christ. This can be seen in Alma's questions: "Have ye spiritually been born of God? Have ye received his image in your countenances?" (Alma 5:14). We usually read *countenance* as referring to the face alone, but in the nineteenth century, it primarily meant "the whole figure or outside appearance."[10] In this way, we can see Alma asking about our being, our way

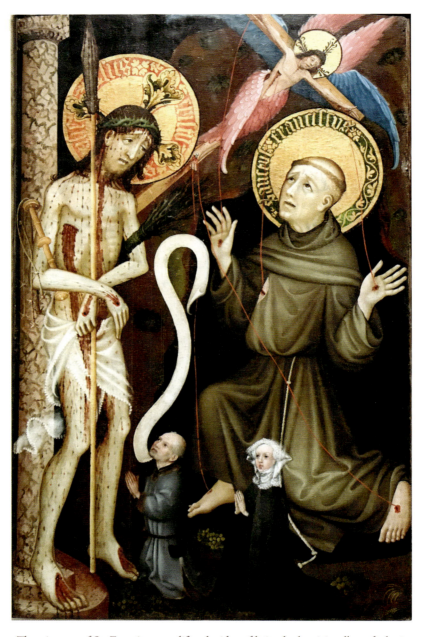

The stigmata of St. Francis exemplifies the idea of being both spiritually and physically changed by following Christ. Christus als Schmerzensmann, hl. Franzikskus und Stifterpaar, around 1420. Wallraf-Richartz-Museum, Köln.

of living. Alma's sense of how deeply our whole selves can be transformed by Christ comes out later in the chapter when he asks, "Can you look up, having the image of God engraven upon your countenances?" (Alma 5:19). The verb *engrave* emphasizes how deeply we can receive Christ's image in our countenance.

Like Francis, Paul also spoke of how he was changed by focusing entirely on Christ, "But God forbid that I should glory, save in the cross of our Lord Jesus Christ, by whom the world is crucified unto me, and I unto the world" (Galatians 6:14). We may not know exactly what he meant, but shortly after this Paul says, "From henceforth let no man trouble me: for I bear in my body the marks of the Lord Jesus" (6:17). The Greek for "marks" is *stigmata*. Paul's body as well as his spirit had come to a knowledge of the Savior.

King Benjamin also teaches how we are changed by serving the Lord. In Mosiah 5 we can see the embodied knowledge that comes through being Christ's servants: "For how knoweth a man the master whom he has not served, and who is a stranger unto him, and is far from the thoughts and intents of his heart?" (Mosiah 5:13). As we seek to follow and serve Christ, we come to know him. Mormon looked ahead to what we can become by continuing on this covenant path. He testified that through this process of becoming true followers of Christ and being filled with his love we take on his image: "when he shall appear we shall be like him for we shall see him as he is; that we may have this hope; that we may be purified even as he is pure" (Moroni 7:48).

President Gordon B. Hinckley taught that our responsibility to take Christ's name and image upon ourselves is not something for a future day. Instead, it is part of our covenant to reflect Christ's image to the world. Our lives and choices must reflect his life and light to the world. "As His followers, we cannot do a mean or shoddy or ungracious thing without tarnishing His image. Nor can we do a good and gracious and generous act without burnishing more brightly the symbol of Him whose name we have taken upon ourselves. And so our lives must become a meaningful expression, the symbol of our declaration of our testimony of the Living

Christ, the Eternal Son of the Living God."[11] Our lives are the symbol of our faith. Part of taking the name of Christ upon us is the responsibility of being a living witness of his living reality.

Ordinances and Embodying Christ

Simply wanting to follow and imitate Christ will not be enough; wanting to know him will not be enough. One of the great blessings of the Restoration is covenant access to Christ's power to transform us. The ordinances show us how and, I believe, enable us to "put on Christ" (Galatians 3:27). Returning to Elder Oaks's words, "The Lord's teachings and teachers were given that we may all attain 'the measure of the stature of the fulness of Christ' (Ephesians 4:13). . . . It is not even enough for us to be convinced of the gospel; we must act and think so that we are converted by it."[12] Having a testimony and feeling Christ's love can convince us of the truthfulness of the gospel, but that kind of knowing will not be enough.

We need to become, and we need power to become more than we are by ourselves. The invitation is to grow into the "measure of the stature of the fulness of Christ." Receiving the ordinances alone cannot substitute for taking on "the measure of the stature of the fulness of Christ" and true conversion, becoming like him, but they do put us on the path. An important way that the ordinances do this is by modeling this new way of being. Additionally, through covenant, the ordinances empower us to become what we promise to become. We can see this ritual embodiment of Christ in baptism and other ordinances.

In the ordinances, we "put on Christ," and participate in his life and his atoning sacrifice. Through our ritual action, we embody how Christ was in the world. We are all familiar with the explanation, clearly elaborated in Paul's writings, that in baptism by immersion we symbolically die, are buried, and are resurrected with Christ.

In Galatians 3:27, Paul says, "For as many of you as have been baptized into Christ have put on Christ." Paul explains how we put on Christ in baptism. When we are "baptized into Jesus Christ [we] were baptized into his death" (Romans 6:3). Our immersion is a participation in his death. Then after "we are buried with him by baptism into death," we also participate in his resurrection, "that like as Christ was raised up from the dead by the glory of the Father, even so we also should walk in newness of life" (Romans 6:4).

The ordinance of baptism allows us to ritually put on Christ. His way of being is modeled in the ordinance of baptism. It is a submission to the will of the Father and a separation from worldliness, the death of the man of sin. The ordinance is not the end but the beginning. Paul tells the saints to live out what they have symbolically done in the ordinance of baptism: "put . . . on the Lord Jesus Christ, and make not provision for the flesh, to fulfil the lusts thereof" (Romans 13:14). We must go forward and walk in newness of life, putting on Christ in our daily life, just as we did in the ordinance.

Another explanation of how ordinances allow us to embody Christ is found in 2 Nephi 31. Nephi explains how the ordinance of baptism is an embodiment of and participation in Christ's life because Christ's own baptism was an embodiment of submission. Christ submitted to immersion and "according to the flesh he [humbled] himself before the Father and [witnessed] unto the Father that he would be obedient unto him in keeping his commandments" (2 Nephi 31:7).

The ordinances are the way in the sense that Christ is the Way. Baptism "showeth unto the children of men the straitness of the path, and the narrowness of the gate, by which they should enter, he having set the example before them" (2 Nephi 31:9). The submission embodied in being immersed in water models an entire life of submission—the life of Christ. "And he said unto the children of men: Follow thou me. Wherefore, my beloved brethren, can we follow Jesus save we shall be willing to keep the commandments of the Father?" (2 Nephi 31:10).

Our ritual embodiment of Christ in baptism continues in the ordinances of the temple. President Harold B. Lee commented, "The receiving of the endowment requires the assuming of obligations by covenants which in reality are but an embodiment or an unfolding of the covenants each person should have assumed at baptism."[13] Through the ordinances, we gain a knowledge of God. Through the ordinances, we ritually embody the kind of obedience and submission that we need to develop in our lives through the process of conversion and becoming.

Charles Wesley, author of so many of our hymns, wrote one of my favorites—"Love Divine, All Loves Excelling"—that does not appear in our hymnbook. For me, the hymn captures the onward progression of coming unto Christ and receiving the power of his Atonement that we experience in the endowment. The words of this hymn often go through my mind during endowment sessions. They illuminate the gradual changes we make as we symbolically come closer and closer to God through the enabling power of Christ.

The first stanza speaks of Christ coming down with redeeming love:

> Love divine, all loves excelling,
> Joy of Heav'n to earth come down;
> Fix in us thy humble dwelling;
> All thy faithful mercies crown!
> Jesus, Thou art all compassion,
> Pure unbounded love Thou art;
> Visit us with Thy salvation,
> Enter every trembling heart.

The following verses express a prayer that Christ "take away the love of sinning" and that we might serve him as his hosts above, never leaving his temple.

The final verse points to the ongoing process through which we come to know Christ as we become like him:

> Finish, then, Thy new creation;
> Pure and spotless let us be;
> Let us see Thy great salvation
> Perfectly restored in Thee;

> Changed from glory into glory,
> 'Til in Heav'n we take our place,
> 'Til we cast our crowns before Thee,
> Lost in wonder, love, and praise.[14]

Becoming transformed into the image of Christ is a process. It is a journey. As we daily repent and exercise our faith in Christ, we are "changed from glory into glory," becoming fit for God's presence. The final result of this process is to receive of his fullness, but, as the book of Revelation says, in that day we will "fall down before him that sat on the throne, and worship him that liveth for ever and ever, and cast [our] crowns before the throne" (4:10). When we finally do arrive, we will truly be "lost in wonder, love, and praise" for his redeeming and exalting love that has re-created us in his image.

Choosing to Know Him

The ordinances point to a way of being in which we know God. They model a way of being in which we have "the mind of Christ" (1 Corinthians 2:16). The knowledge of God that the ordinances allow us to experience through ritual embodiment leads us to a new kind of life. This is a life in which we know Christ because his Spirit is in us, helping us to want and to do what Christ would want and do. As we live out our covenants, we come to know Christ. We learn what to do, what to say, and how to live in a holy and godly manner. Through obedience and submission in ritual action, we both consent to be and learn to be in the world as Christ was. In the ordinances, we come to know Christ because we "put on Christ" through ritual embodiment (see Galatians 3:27). We participate in an embodiment of submission and willingness to obey as he did. It is not an abstract knowledge of Christ but an embodied knowledge.

The ordinances are necessary but not sufficient. We make covenants, but we also must choose to keep those covenants. We "put on Christ" in the ordinances, but we must also "put on Christ" in our lives. The covenant to obey becomes meaningful not if we see it as an obligation to save ourselves, but when we see it as a choice to more fully receive Christ into our lives. In the ordinances, we embody his submission, his obedience.

We learn to take his name and his nature upon ourselves. Christ said, "Come unto me, all ye that labour and are heavy laden, and I will give you rest. Take my yoke upon you, and learn of me; for I am meek and lowly in heart: and ye shall find rest unto your souls. For my yoke is easy, and my burden is light" (Matthew 11:28–30). When we see the ordinances' ritual embodiment of Christ as the means of accepting this invitation, then obedience in *all* aspects of our lives makes sense in light of the gospel. Obedience is not about our capacity but our willingness.

Obedience is the choice to exercise faith and submit. The submission of our will, as Elder Neal A. Maxwell so often emphasized, is the one thing we have to offer.[15] Our submission to the will of the Father is the only way we can put on Christ. In our echo of "thy will, not mine be done," we connect ourselves with the grace of Christ. "Abide in me, and I in you. As the branch cannot bear fruit of itself, except it abide in the vine; no more can ye, except ye abide in me. I am the vine, ye are the branches: He that abideth in me, and I in him, the same bringeth forth much fruit: for without me ye can do nothing" (John 15:4–5). Putting on Christ through participating in his ordinances is accepting the invitation to know God. The ritual embodiment of Christ is accepting the invitation to eternal life because it is Christ's life, God's life, that we are choosing to receive.

The connection of further ordinances and the knowledge of God is made explicit in Doctrine and Covenants, section 84. "And this greater priesthood administereth the gospel and holdeth the key of the mysteries of the kingdom, even the key of the knowledge of God" (84:19) As we seek to know Christ, we must look for this knowledge in the temple ordinances of the Melchizedek Priesthood. "Therefore, in the ordinances thereof, the power of godliness is manifest" (84:20).

The ritual embodiment of the ordinances points to and empowers us for the true embodiment and true knowledge that comes through personal conversion and sanctification. "And without the ordinances thereof, and the authority of the priesthood, the power of godliness is not manifest unto men in the flesh; For without this no man can see the face of God, even the Father, and live" (Doctrine and Covenants 84:21–22). The endowment of power gives us hope that we can gradually come to know Christ. It gives us hope that we can return to his presence and receive the kind of life that he has. As we accept the invitation to "come unto Christ, and be perfected in him," we come to know him as we become like him (Moroni 10:32–33; see Moroni 7:48).

A Renewed Invitation

When my husband and I moved to California to start doctoral work, we had a chance to live for a year in my grandfather's house in Pasadena, in the stake where President Howard W. Hunter had been stake president. My grandfather had passed away the previous year, shortly after we were married, but the house was still owned by the family and it was a blessing to feel connected to family during that transition in our lives.

My grandfather had served on the high council under President Hunter decades before I was born, but I had heard my mother speak about it on occasion. A couple of months before we moved to Pasadena, Ezra Taft Benson passed away and President Hunter became the prophet. During the time he was prophet, President Hunter was not able to travel very much, but he did arrange to come to Pasadena. My husband and I had a chance to sing in the choir when he spoke at our stake conference, and we felt his spirit of love and his vision for the Church. Hearing him in person somehow magnified the words that he gave in his other addresses as prophet.

President Hunter was not President of the Church for even one full year. His life had been preserved, and he seemed to have one subject to talk about that everyone would hear: the temple. We also heard his invitation to "live with ever more attention to the life and example of the Lord Jesus Christ," but may not have realized how interwoven that was with his invitation that all be worthy of a temple recommend and attend the temple as often as circumstances permit.

In his very first general conference talk as prophet, President Hunter expressed a piercing vision of the temple as a symbol of our membership. With it, he extended an invitation to "study the Master's every teaching and devote ourselves more fully to his example."[16] He explained that Christ "has given us 'all things that pertain unto life and godliness.' He has 'called us to glory and virtue' and has 'given unto us exceeding great and precious promises: that by these [we] might be partakers of the divine nature' (2 Pet. 1:3–4)." President Hunter gave his witness of those promises that Peter spoke of. "I believe in those 'exceeding great and precious promises,' and I invite all within the sound of my voice to claim them. We should strive to 'be partakers of the divine nature.'" President Hunter continued, "In that spirit I invite the Latter-day Saints to look to the temple of the Lord as the great symbol of your membership."

With this insight from a modern prophet we can look at this passage in 2 Peter and see more clearly the relationship between the temple and coming to know and become like Christ. We read in 2 Peter that Christ's "divine power hath given unto us all things that pertain unto life and godliness, *through the knowledge of him* that hath called us to glory and virtue: Whereby are given unto us exceeding great and precious promises: *that by these* ye might be partakers of the divine nature" (1:3–4; emphasis added). President Hunter could see that we become partakers of the divine nature *through* the great and precious promises we receive in the temple. He could see that it was only "by these" covenant promises that we could get the "divine power" that we need to change and become what we need to become. It is only by putting on Christ through the ordinances of the temple that we come to know him. It is only by putting on Christ through the ordinances of the temple that we receive "all things that pertain unto life and godliness."

The promises through which we become "partakers of the divine nature" are the promises in the ordinances and covenants of the temple. These promises are the way that we come to know Christ. It is only by making and keeping these covenants that we are able to receive these great and precious promises that allow us to be partakers of the divine nature. "This greater priesthood administereth the gospel and holdeth the key of the mysteries of the kingdom, even the key of the knowledge of God. Therefore, in the ordinances thereof, the power of godliness is manifest" (Doctrine and Covenants 84:19–20). Through the ordinances we receive the power to become godly.

Assisting people to come to a knowledge of God seems to be the very purpose for which the Restoration was brought about. Some may look back to the early days of the Restoration with nostalgia and long for a time when knowledge was poured out on the Saints. I believe that such a view rests on a limited understanding of knowledge.

With a broader sense of knowledge as embodied, both in ordinance and in converted lives, I believe that now is the time when the knowledge of God is positioned to be poured out more than at any other time in history. I believe that through the expansion of the Church and the building of temples throughout the earth, we are seeing the beginning of the fulfillment of Jeremiah's prophecy.

> Behold, the days come, saith the Lord, that I will make a new covenant with the house of Israel. . . . After those days, saith the Lord, *I will put my law in their inward parts, and write it in their hearts*; and will be their God, and they shall be my people. And *they shall teach no more every man his neighbour, and every man his brother, saying, Know the Lord: for they shall all know me*, from the least of them unto the greatest of them, saith the Lord; for I will forgive their iniquity, and I will remember their sin no more. (Jeremiah 31:31–34; emphasis added)

Elder Oaks observes that "in contrast to the institutions of the world, which teach us to know something, the gospel of Jesus Christ challenges us to become something." As Latter-day Saints we should not look only for intellectual knowledge that comes in a form understandable to the "institutions of the world," even if it were to include information that we may feel we need to respond to questions about or criticisms of the Church. We should not be disheartened because there are not new sections added to the Doctrine and Covenants.

The knowledge of God is available. The "key of the knowledge of God" has been restored (Doctrine and Covenants 84:19). "Therefore, in the ordinances thereof, the power of godliness is manifest" (84:20). The ordinances were "given that we may all attain 'the measure of the stature of the fulness of Christ.'" As we live out our covenants, we grow into that knowledge. As we attain the "stature of the fulness of Christ" (Ephesians 4:13), we will know God because we will have become like him (see 1 John 3:1–6; Moroni 7:48).

NOTES

1. Some components of this chapter on embodied knowledge appeared earlier in my "Embodied Knowledge of God," *Element: A Journal of Mormon Philosophy and Theology* 2, no. 1 (2006): 61–71. Other sections on St. Francis appeared earlier in my "I Am among You as One That Serveth," *Element: A Journal of Mormon Philosophy and Theology* 5, no. 2 (2009): 57–67.
2. Dallin H. Oaks, "The Challenge to Become," *Ensign*, November 2000, 32.
3. Thomas of Celano, *The Life of Saint Francis*, in *The Francis Trilogy*, ed. Regis J. Armstrong, J. A. Wayne Hellmann, and William J. Short (Hyde Park, NY: New City Press), 58.
4. Thomas of Celmo, *Life of Saint Francis*, 88.
5. Bonaventure, *Legenda maior*, or "The Life of St. Francis," in *The Soul's Journey into God, The Tree of Life, The Life of St. Francis*, trans. Ewert Cousins (Mahwah, NJ: Paulist Press, 1978), 218.
6. Bonaventure, *Legenda maior*, 239.
7. Bonaventure, *Legenda maior*, 245.
8. Bonaventure, *Legenda maior*, 190.
9. Bonaventure, *Legenda maior*, 305.
10. *An American Dictionary of the English Language* (New York: Johnson Reprint, 1970), s.v. "Countenance."

11. Gordon B. Hinckley, "The Symbol of Our Faith," *Ensign*, April 2005, 3.

12. Oaks, "Challenge to Become," 32.

13. *The Teachings of Harold B. Lee: Eleventh President of The Church of Jesus Christ of Latter-day Saints*, ed. Clyde J. Williams (Salt Lake City: Bookcraft, 1996), 574.

14. Charles Wesley, "Love Divine, All Loves Excelling," in *Hymns for the Family of God* (Nashville, TN: Paragon Associates, 1976), no. 21.

15. See, for example, Neal A. Maxwell, "Willing to Submit," *Ensign*, May 1985, 70–71.

16. Howard W. Hunter, "Exceeding Great and Precious Promises," *Ensign*, November 1994, 8.

"Look unto me in every thought; doubt not, fear not. Behold the wounds which pierced my side, and also the prints of the nails in my hands and feet" (Doctrine and Covenants 6:36–37). The Prayer Book of Bonne of Luxembourg, Duchess of Normandy, fol. 328r, before 1349. The Metropolitan Museum of Art, New York, The Cloisters Collection, 1969.

PART THREE

CONCLUSION

"I am the vine, ye are the branches: He that abideth in me, and I in him, the same bringeth forth much fruit: for without me ye can do nothing" (John 15:5). Door Post with Grapevine Emerging from a Chalice, *sixth–seventh century. The Metropolitan Museum of Art, New York, Rogers Fund, 1910.*

CHAPTER 15

COVENANTS AND THE TRUE VINE

e are all on a journey in life. Each day moves us forward in becoming more of the person we are choosing to become. This process is inevitable and relentless. For many people this can feel like a depressing downward slide, a "Long Day's Journey into Night"[1] in which we find ourselves trapped by our weaknesses and those of others. Christ invites us to follow a different trajectory. He promised, "If ye continue in my word, then are ye my disciples indeed; and ye shall know the truth, and the truth shall make you free" (John 8:31–32). The greatest truth to know is the truth of Christ's role as our Redeemer. He is the Father's plan. He is the Way, the Truth, and the Life. The only way to find the freedom that he offers is to continue in his word, becoming his disciples and coming to know him as we experience the freedom of living his kind of life.

The redemption price that he offers is a gift. Through the ransom price of his atoning sacrifice, Christ is offering us a way to change course.

He is offering us a way to walk his covenant path, to come unto him by receiving his Atonement in ordinances and converted lives. God himself came down to atone for the sins of the world, but we decide if we want to give away our sins to know him. The great Jehovah gave himself to free us from the bondage of sin and our fallen state, but we decide if we are willing to make and keep the covenants that he offers us. Christ's Atonement is the ransom price, but redemption happens only when we receive that gift. We decide if we want to leave the prison.

The restoration of Christ's Church reestablished the only path back home. Knowing about the gospel isn't enough. We need to make and keep covenants to take upon ourselves the name of Christ and thereby to receive his nature. With the restoration of the priesthood, we can receive power with every covenant that we make and keep.

The ordinances present us with images and representations of his suffering and death. Taking time to slow down and reverently behold the sacrifice of the Lamb of God in these symbols, we realize that we are being offered tangible connections to Christ's redeeming love. Partaking of this gift can move us to humility and gratitude, giving us courage to continue along the covenant path. As we prioritize scripture study and participation in the ordinances, seeking to behold and respond to Christ's redeeming suffering and death, we can feel the love and grace that "so freely he offers [us]." As we see and respond to his mercy and love, we can "tremble to know that for me he was crucified, that for me a sinner he suffered and bled and died."[2] As we behold the wounds that pierced his side, and the prints of the nails in his hands and his feet, we can gain the faith and hope to enter into and stay on the only path forward, the only path home.

We cannot be where he is and stay where we are. We cannot become as he is and stay as we are. But the good news is that, thanks to Christ's ransom, the covenant path will take us there. Christ will take us there. That is the promise. That is *his* promise.

Understanding that the covenants are not a superpromise that we can never fulfill but, instead, a new relationship in which Christ becomes our Kinsman-Redeemer can give us courage to stay on the covenant path. We won't make it on our own—we can't make it on our own. But we don't have to. That is why we have a Redeemer. His grace is sufficient. His power will continue to lift us and inspire us to keep making changes, to keep growing, to keep healing, to keep becoming more and more godly, but we must keep our covenants to keep that power in our lives.

In the Sermon on the Mount, Christ said, "Consider the lilies of the field, how they grow" (Matthew 6:28). It sounds effortless when he says "they toil not, neither do they spin," but I wonder if he might be using the growth of plants as a symbol, a way to understand the growth and life that the new and everlasting covenant offers. Our bondage lies in our hearts and minds. We do what we want, and so if we are not wanting what God wants, the problem is how to change what we want.

Christ offers us a radical solution—to connect ourselves to him through covenant and to receive him through the ordinances, and then let his power and Spirit change our desires. As we draw near unto him and receive his grace, our natures develop and change as surely as lilies do grow. Christ says, "I am the vine, ye are the branches: He that abideth in me, and I in him, the same bringeth forth much fruit: for without me ye can do nothing" (John 15:5). I know of no better explanation for the power of the covenant path. Covenants are Christ's way of inviting us to connect to the source of life so that we can bring forth fruit and have his power in our lives—in the ordinances thereof, the power of godliness is manifest. Consider the lilies of the field, consider the branches on the vine, how they grow, how they bring forth much fruit.

When we choose to connect ourselves to Christ through covenant we become free. We accept him as our Redeemer and he takes us on the journey from bondage. The irony of the covenant freedom that Christ offers is that this freedom is the strait and narrow path and that the bondage was our life of willfulness and living our way, what we thought was freedom. This covenant freedom brings us into closer and closer alignment with his will, just as he lived in perfect alignment with the Father's will. The freedom to bring forth much fruit and to be filled with the desire to do good and be good flows from being connected to the True Vine. Christ offers us a covenant relationship so that we can experience a new kind of life, a life full of his Spirit. Resisting covenant requirements is resisting the very connection to Christ's life that will allow us to be as the lilies of the field and the branches on the grapevine. We can grow. We will grow. The lily doesn't toil or spin. The lily grows. The branch of the grapevine doesn't punch a time card—it brings forth much fruit.

Covenants are organic. They connect us to Christ. He is the light and the life of the world. He wants us to have his light and his power, now and throughout all eternity. He stands waiting to give us this light and power, to infuse our lives with new desires and loving feelings. The gift of the Holy Ghost is the most precious gift that Christ's Atonement makes possible in this life. The covenants and ordinances are our lifeline. Making and keeping covenants helps us tap into the source of life, today and forever. Participating in the ordinances allows us to behold and receive the atoning death that is the source of our eternal life. Through the covenants and ordinances, Christ allows us to come to know him as we receive his name, his nature.

I experienced this myself when I was nearing my twentieth birthday. It was a Sunday afternoon in fall, and the semester was not going well. My life was not going well. Something inside me offered a prayer for help, and then I lay down on my dorm room bed and took a nap. When I awoke, a phrase from the last general conference came into my mind. President Ezra Taft Benson had promised that when you put God first, everything will fall into place or fall out of your life. That thought was a seed that I had to decide whether to cultivate or not. Maybe I felt I had nothing to lose. Maybe I was just desperate enough to try anything. But something inside me trusted that this was real, that this would work. So I started.

I started right then thinking about what it meant to put God first in my life. I knew it meant I needed to do the things that I knew I should be doing but wasn't. I knew that I should pray, not only before I went to sleep but also in the morning. So I changed that. I knew that I should attend my Sunday School class and not wander around and talk with my hallmates. So I changed that. I knew that President Benson was teaching that we should read the Book of Mormon every day. I did read my scriptures every day, but not the Book of Mormon. So I changed that.

Putting the Lord first was exercising my faith unto repentance. Putting the Lord first was choosing to keep my covenants. As I started making these choices, I started feeling and recognizing promptings from the Holy Ghost in a way that I never had before. As I started reading the Book of Mormon and listening to the promptings of the Spirit, I realized that I needed to choose to receive the gift that had been promised me in my confirmation many years before. As I more actively sought to receive the Holy Ghost, I started getting impressions about other things I needed to change. Step by step, I moved forward on the journey out of bondage and into the freedom of discipleship. I began that journey over thirty years ago, and I have been on it ever since.

I know that Christ is our Redeemer because I know that he is my Redeemer. Like the man born blind, I can say, "One thing I know, that, whereas I was blind, now I see" (John 9:25). I know that making and keeping our covenants is the journey of receiving the blessings of Christ's atoning sacrifice. The ordinances point the way and mark the path of how to receive his nature, the divine nature. As we come unto him on that journey, we come to know for ourselves that he is come that we might have life and that we might have it more abundantly.

I know for myself that if we look we will live. I know that as we believe on his name we will repent of all our sins. This is the covenant path. I know that as we come unto Christ we can be perfected in him. This is the journey of faith in the Lord Jesus Christ: covenanting to take his name upon us, becoming the children of the covenant, and then moving forward to live lives of worship, bowing down and serving him with lives of obedience and sacrifice. As we press forward, our outward service gradually becomes inward sanctification; we increasingly seek for the holiness of his presence and deny ourselves of all ungodliness.

Through the Restoration, the power of godliness is made available through the ordinances of salvation. Christ manifests his ransom price to us through the immersion of baptism and the emblems of the sacrament. He invites us to participate, to partake. As we slow down to behold, we likewise see in the symbols of the endowment and sealing Christ's gift of life. He invites us to fully take his name and nature upon us, to respond to the gift of his sacrifice with our lives of sacrifice and consecration. We can move forward with hope. We can move forward with humility, knowing that we are saved only in and through his atoning blood. He is the vine, and we are the branches.

We can move forward and grow upward, gradually becoming partakers of his divine nature through the "great and precious promises" of our covenant relationship (see 2 Peter 1:3–4). We can doubt not and fear not as we behold his wounds and trust in his redeeming blood. "His way is the path that leads to happiness in this life and eternal life in the world to come. God be thanked for the matchless gift of His divine Son."[3] Because of the Father's plan of redemption and Christ's gift of his life, we can receive life. We can be connected to the True Vine and have that life flowing through us now and forever.

NOTES

1. Title of a play by Eugene O'Neill.
2. Charles H. Gabriel, "I Stand All Amazed," in *Hymns* (Salt Lake City: The Church of Jesus Christ of Latter-day Saints, 1985), no. 193.
3. "The Living Christ: The Testimony of the Apostles," *Ensign*, April 2000, 2.

FOR FURTHER READING

or those interesting in exploring the scholarship of the ancient words I develop in this volume, my publications through the years may be a starting place. In addition to more in-depth analysis of these ancient words, the footnotes point to many other scholars' insights on these topics.

"The Lord Will Redeem His People: Adoptive Covenant and Redemption in the Old Testament and Book of Mormon." *Journal of Book of Mormon Studies* 2, no. 2 (1993): 39–62.

"The Lord Will Redeem His People: 'Adoptive' Covenant and Redemption in the Old Testament." In *Thy People Shall Be My People and Thy God My God*, edited by Paul Y. Hoskisson, 49–60. Salt Lake City: Deseret Book, 1993; or "The Lord Will Redeem His People: Adoptive Covenant and Redemption in the Old Testament." In *Sperry Symposium Classics: The Old Testament*, edited by Paul Y. Hoskisson,

298–310. Provo, UT: Religious Studies Center, Brigham Young University; Salt Lake City: Deseret Book, 2005.

"Hebrew Concepts of Adoption and Redemption in the Writings of Paul." In *The Apostle Paul: His Life and His Testimony*, edited by Paul Y. Hoskisson, 80–95. Salt Lake City: Deseret Book, 1994.

"The Redemption of Abraham." In *Astronomy, Papyrus, and Covenant*, edited by John Gee and Brian M. Hauglid, 167–74. Studies in the Book of Abraham 3. Provo, UT: Institute for the Study and Preservation of Ancient Religious Texts, 2005.

"Choosing Redemption." In *Living the Book of Mormon: 'Abiding by Its Precepts,'* edited by Charles Swift and Gaye Strathearn, 163–75. Salt Lake City: Deseret Book, 2007.

"Redemption's Grand Design for the Living and the Dead." In *The Doctrine and Covenants: Revelations in Context*, edited by Andrew H. Hedges, J. Spencer Fluhman, and Alonzo Gaskill, 188–211. Salt Lake City: Deseret Book, 2008.

"The Presence of God." In *The Things Which My Father Saw: Approaches to Lehi's Dream and Nephi's Vision*, edited by Daniel L. Belnap, Gaye Strathearn, and Stanley A. Johnson, 119–34. Provo, UT: Religious Studies Center, Brigham Young University; Salt Lake City: Deseret Book, 2011.

"Worship: Bowing Down and Serving the Lord." In *Ascending the Mountain of the Lord: Temple, Praise, and Worship in the Old Testament*, edited by David Rolph Seely, Jeffrey R. Chadwick, and Matthew J. Grey, 122–35. Provo, UT: Religious Studies Center, Brigham Young University; Salt Lake City: Deseret Book, 2013.

"Healing, Wholeness, and Repentance in Acts 3." In *The Ministry of Peter, the Chief Apostle*, edited by Frank F. Judd, Eric D. Huntsman, and Shon D. Hopkin, 151–68. Provo, UT: Religious Studies Center, Brigham Young University; Salt Lake City: Deseret Book, 2014.

"Sitting Enthroned: A Scriptural Perspective," *Religious Educator* 19, no. 1 (2018): 103–17.

On medieval images and the theology of Christ's atonement, I have written:

"*Compassio*: Participation in the Passion and Late Medieval Jerusalem Pilgrimage." PhD dissertation, Claremont Graduate University, 2002.

"'Come Follow Me': The Imitation of Christ in the Later Middle Ages." In *Prelude to the Restoration: From Apostasy to the Restored Church*, edited by Steven C. Harper et al., 115–29. Provo, UT: Religious Studies Center, Brigham Young University; Salt Lake City: Deseret Book, 2004.

"Embodied Knowledge of God." *Element: A Journal of Mormon Philosophy and Theology* 2, no. 1 (2006): 61–71.

"The Whole Meaning of the Law: Christ's Vicarious Sacrifice." In *The Gospel of Jesus Christ in the Old Testament*, edited by D. Kelly Ogden, Jared W. Ludlow, and Kerry Muhlestein, 68–87. Provo, UT: Religious Studies Center, Brigham Young University; Salt Lake City: Deseret Book, 2009.

"I Am among You as One That Serveth." *Element: A Journal of Mormon Philosophy and Theology* 5, no. 2 (2009): 57–67.

"Seeking the Sacred: Replicating the Holy Sepulchre and Jerusalem Pilgrimage." In *Seek Ye Words of Wisdom: Studies of the Book of Mormon, Bible, and Temple in Honor of Stephen D. Ricks*, edited by Donald W. Parry, Gaye Strathearn, Shon D. Hopkin, 367–83. Provo, UT: Interpreter Foundation and Religious Education, Brigham Young University, 2019.

INDEX

A

ʿābad (serve), 37, 42. See also service
Abinadi, 19–20
Abrahamic covenant, 21–23
Abram / Abraham, 9–10
Adam, 78
agency, 15, 127
Alma the Younger, 141–42, 157–59
Arma Christi, 109–12. See also Man of Sorrows
    and pondering suffering of Christ, 112–14
    and receiving Atonement, 116–17
    and slowing down to behold Christ's suffering, 114–16
asceticism, 155–57
Atonement
    as available to all, 17–18
    gaining testimony of, 152
    need for, 31–32
    ordinances point to, 78–79, 174
    presence of Lord made accessible through, 58
    receiving, 116–17, 120–21, 174
    redemption through, 151–52
Augustine, 112

B

baptism, 7, 12–13, 14, 160–61
become / becoming, 67–68, 153–54, 157, 160
Benedictine monks, 99–100
Benedict XVI, Pope, 153–54
Benjamin, King, 10, 141, 159
Benson, Ezra Taft, 11–12, 90–91, 176, 177
běrît (covenant), 8. See also covenants
Bernard of Clairvaux, 132–33
bitter cup, 127
Bonaventure, 155–57
bondage
    escaping, 33–34, 73, 175
    of Israelites, 23, 24–27, 34
    under Mosaic law, 37
    redemption from, 18–19
Book of Mormon
    concept of looking to Redeemer in, 24–26
    memorizing verses from, 11–12
    teachings on God's presence in, 56–57
    textual responses to Christ in, 140–42
"bow down," 37–38, 39–41, 42

INDEX

C

carcass, parable of, 105
cathedrals, 96–97
change
    belief in possibility of, 16
    in covenant relationship, 13
    through Jesus Christ, 157–59, 175
    and "song of redeeming love," 33
change of heart, 142
charity, 71
children of God, 145–46
Christus Victor theory, 107n3
Church of Jesus Christ of Latter-day Saints, The, controversies concerning, 40–41
Cistercians, 132–33
compassion
    for Christ's suffering, 131
    Pietà as model of, 134–38
confidence
    through covenants, 14, 27–29, 178
    in Jesus Christ, 14, 15–16, 29–32, 40–41, 68, 85–87, 178
Constantinople, passion relics from, 103
controversies, faith through, 40–41
countenance, 157–59
covenants, 7–9
    confidence through, 14, 27–30
    connecting to Christ through, 175–76
    courage through, 174–75
    and family relationships, 8–11, 26
    as lifeline, 176
    power through, 174
    putting on Christ through, 163–64
    and submission in worship, 40
    taking hold of, 52–53
    and taking upon name of Christ, 11–13
    trust in, 70
    and understanding identity, 11, 14–16
crown of thorns, 102–3
crucifixion. See *Arma Christi*; Atonement; Man of Sorrows; passion piety; passion relics; suffering
crusaders, 101
crying, over love for Savior, 129–30

D

death, spiritual, 55
differences, and presence of Lord, 53–54
divine nature, 71
Dominican movement, 99, 101
doubt, 151

E

embodied knowledge, 154, 157, 159
embodiment of image of Christ, 155–60
endowment, 116–17, 165
Eucharist, 99, 120–21. *See also* sacrament
eunuchs, 51–52
exaltation, 71–74

F

faith
    hope as fruit of, 70
    in Jesus Christ, 14, 15–16, 29–32, 40–41, 68
    replacing doubt with, 151
    using art as reminder of, 91
    using art to increase, 88–89
    using art to show, 89–91
fallen selves, 64
family relationships, and covenants, 8–11, 26
Franciscan movement, 99, 101
Francis of Assisi, St., 155–57
freedom, 35–36, 175–76

G

gā'al (redeem), 21
garments of righteousness, putting on, 72–74
gathering of Saints, 105
gifts, accepting, 119–20
glory, worthiness to inherit throne of, 64–65
God
    putting, first, 176–77
    wrath of, 126–28

God, presence of
  experiencing, continually, 56–58
  holiness and, 47–49
  invitation into, 54–56
  joy in, 58–60
  seeking out, 45–47
  and symbols of holiness in temple worship, 49–54
gō'ēl (kinsman-redeemer), 21–22. See also Redeemer, Jesus Christ as,
gold plates, 24–25
growth, spiritual, 175, 176

H

Hafen, Bruce C., 117
Hafen, Marie K., 117
Handel's *Messiah*, 116–17
Hannah, 64
happiness. *See* joy
healing, 85–87, 121
heart
  change of, 142
  hardened, 130–31
Hinckley, Gordon B., 159–60
history, relics as physical connections to, 103–4
holiness
  happiness through, 59–60
  and presence of Lord, 47–49, 52–53, 55–56, 58
Holy Ghost, 57, 59
hope, 16, 24, 29, 30, 69, 70, 79–80
"How Firm a Foundation," 30
Hunter, Howard W., 165–66
ḥwh / ḥwy (bow down), 37, 42. *See also* "bow down"

I

"I Believe in Christ," 4
iconoclasm, 3n2, 87, 89–90
identity, covenants and understanding, 11, 14–16
idol worship, 88
Imago pietatis. *See* Man of Sorrows
impurity, ritual, 51–52
invitations, accepting, 119–20

Israelites, 10, 21–27, 34, 37, 42, 49–52, 78

J

Jensen, Virginia U., 90
Jerusalem, passion relics from, 101–2
Jesus Christ. *See also Arma Christi*; Atonement; God, presence of; winepress
  access to presence of God through, 52
  author receives witness of, 3–4
  becoming like, 71, 155–60
  becoming peaceable followers of, 69–70
  being settled in love and covenant promises of, 69–71
  change in medieval perceptions and depictions of, 98–99
  change through, 157–59, 175
  compassion for suffering of, 131–34
  connecting to, through covenants, 175–76
  crying over love for, 129–30
  dual nature of, 146–52
  embodiment of image of, 155–60
  as exemplar, 39–41
  faith, trust, and confidence in, 14, 15–16, 29–32, 40–41, 68, 85–87, 178
  as foundation, 66–67
  image of, engraved on countenance, 157–59
  images of, 85–92
  looking to, 24–27, 33, 92
  love of, 65–67
  models of love for, 138–40
  ordinances and embodying, 160–63
  ordinances as means of knowing, 163–65, 168
  pondering suffering of, 112–14
  as Ransom, 77–80
  as Redeemer, 19–24, 77–80, 173, 175, 177
  remembering, 38, 92
  repentance made possible through, 64
  sacrament as connection to, 105–6
  serving, 36–39
  sitting down with, 71–74

INDEX

Jesus Christ (*continued*)
    slowing down to behold suffering of, 114–16
    submission of, 161
    submission to, 35–36
    taking upon name of, 10, 11–13, 14–15, 58, 159–60, 164
    temple and coming to know and become like, 165–68
    textual responses to, 140–42
    as way to heavenly life, 63
joy
    through holiness, 59–60
    in Lord's presence, 58–60
    as nature of God, 59
judgment, 126–28

K

Kirtland Temple, 14
knowledge
    and becoming, 153–54, 157
    embodied, 154, 157, 159
    through ordinances, 154–55
    through temple worship, 165–68

L

Lee, Harold B., 161–62
Lehi, 24, 47
Levites, 42
life
    pleasure and holiness in, 48–49
    as worship, 43–44
Life of Christ, 101
Long Medford, England, church floor, 90
love
    crying over, for Savior, 129–30
    of Jesus Christ, 65–67
    Mary as model of, 138–40
    sitting down in, 62–63
"Love Divine, All Loves Excelling," 162–63

M

Man of Sorrows, 146–52

martyrs, graves of, 95–96
Mary
    compassion of, 134–38
    as model of love, 138–40
    rise of devotion to, 99
Mass, embodied knowledge in ritual actions of, 153–54
Maxwell, Neal A., 133, 164
Meditationes vitae Christi, 131–32
mercy, 67–68
Messiah (Handel), 116–17
Michelangelo, 135–36
miracle of water turned to wine at Cana, 123–24
monastic reform movements, 99–101
Mormon, 159
Moroni, 71–72
Mosaic law, 22–24, 37, 42, 49–52, 53, 78
Moses, 10, 34

N

name
    covenants and new, 9–10
    taking upon Christ's, 10, 11–13, 14–15, 58, 159–60, 164
nativity scenes and sets, 90
natural man, 27–29, 30–31, 128
Nelson, Russell M., 121
Nephi, 24–26, 27–29, 79, 115–16
numbness, spiritual, 130–31

O

Oaks, Dallin H., 154, 160, 167
obedience, 38–39, 43–44, 56–57, 163–64
Old Testament
    author's academic study of redemption in, 5–6
    presence of God in, 47–48
    redemption in, 19, 21–23
    worship in, 42
olive oil, 121
"Once in David's Royal City," 20
ordinances
    and embodying Christ, 160–63
    as lifeline, 176

as means for knowing God and
    Christ, 163–65, 168
as means of conveying knowledge,
    154–55
point to Christ's sacrifice, 78–79, 174
power of godliness available through,
    178

P

pādāh (redeem), 21
pānîm (presence of the Lord), 47. See
    also God, presence of
parable of carcass, 105
passion piety, 99. See also Arma Christi
passion relics, 101–3. See also Arma
    Christi
patrons, 96, 98
Paul, 159
pelican, legend of, 125–26
Pietà, 134–40
Pietà (Michelangelo), 135–36
pilgrims, 101
plan of salvation, 77–78
"Poor Wayfaring Man of Grief, A," 3
poverty, 155–57
pride, 32
priesthood, 10, 15, 40–41
purity, ritual, 51–52

R

Ransom, Jesus Christ as, 77–80
rebirth, spiritual, 145–46
reconciliation, 85–87
Redeemer, Jesus Christ as, 19–24,
    77–80, 173, 175, 177
redemption. See also salvation
    author's academic study of, 5–6
    as available to all, 17–18
    and belonging to Christ, 35–36
    Book of Mormon teachings on,
        24–26
    defined, 18
    miracle at Cana as foreshadowing,
        123–24
    in Old Testament, 19, 21–23
    receiving, 173–74

recognizing need for, 31–32
rejecting, 54–55, 119–20
remembering our personal, 27–29
from slavery, 18–19
and "song of redeeming love," 32–34
through Jesus Christ, 19–24
trust and belief in, 113–14
and trust in Jesus Christ, 29–32
red garments, 120
Reformation, 89–90, 93n3
relics, 95–96
passion relics, 101–3
as physical connections to history,
    103–4
and sacrament as connection to
    Christ, 105–6
spread of, throughout Europe, 96–101
reliquaries, 102
remembrance, 38, 91, 92
repentance, 62–63, 64
Restoration, 83, 133, 160, 174
resurrection, 112, 146–52
"Reverently and Meekly Now," 113, 123
Ricks, Stephen, 5
ritual purity and impurity, 51–52
robe of righteousness, putting on, 72–74

S

sacrament, 87, 105–6, 120–21. See also
    Eucharist
sacrament hymns, 113, 122–23
sacrament prayers, 15, 38
Sacred Grove, 103
sacrifices, 78
Sainte-Chappelle, 102–3
Saint-Étienne Cathedral (Limoges), 97
Saint-Front Cathedral (Périgueux), 97
Saints, gathering of, 105
salvation. See also redemption
    Christus Victor theory of, 107n3
    and redemption in Old Testament, 19
    sacrament as connection to, 105–6
sanctification, 59, 60
scriptures, textual responses to Christ
    in, 140–42. See also Book of
    Mormon; Old Testament
Second Coming, 120
seed, Alma's parable of, 150

INDEX

service
- and becoming like Christ, 155
- desire to render, 63–64
- worship and, 36–39, 43–44

Seven Sorrows of Mary, 134–35
signs, functioning of *Arma Christi* as, 111–12
Simeon, 135
Simon, 130–31
sincerity, 68
sitting enthroned, 61–66
- and being settled in Christ's love and covenant promises, 69–71
- and Christ's redeeming love as foundation, 66–67
- and invitation to become, 67–68
- and sitting down with Jesus Christ, 71–74

slavery. *See* bondage
Small Calvary, The, 124
"song of redeeming love," 32–34
spiritual death, 55
spiritual growth, 175, 176
spiritual numbness, 130–31
spiritual rebirth, 145–46
spirit world, 55
stigmata, 157, 159
submission, 35–36, 38, 39–41, 43, 161, 164
suffering. *See also Arma Christi*; winepress
- compassion for Christ's, 131–34
- finding comfort in Christ's, 109–10
- interdependence of Christ's resurrection and, 146–52
- Pietà as model of response to, 134–38
- pondering Christ's, 112–14
- seeking out, 132–34
- slowing down to behold Christ's, 114–16

T

tāmîm (perfect / whole), 50
temple worship
- among Israelites and latter-day Saints, 42–43
- and being clothed with righteousness, 73
- coming to know and be like Christ through, 165–68
- and meaning of endowment, 116–17
- and presence of Lord, 47–48
- priesthood and, 41
- putting on Christ through, 161–63
- symbolism of holiness in, 49–54
- worthiness for, 54

Ten Commandments, 37, 38
Thomas of Celano, 155
transubstantiation, 99

V

van der Weyden, Rogier, 134, 136–38
Vita Christi, 101

W

Washington D.C. Temple, 119
water, in sacrament, 122–24
weaknesses, 27–29, 30–31, 65–66, 71–72
wedding at Cana, 123–24
Wesley, Charles, 162–63
wine, 122–25
winepress, 120–28
"witness trees," 103
worship. *See also* temple worship
- life as, 43–44
- and serving Lord, 36–39
- submission in, 35–36, 38, 39–41
- in temple, 42–43

worthiness, for temple worship, 54
wrath of God, 126–28

Y

yašab (sit down, sit enthroned), 61. *See also* sitting enthroned